# THE
# COMPASSION
# FATIGUE
# WORKBOOK

Creative Tools for Transforming Compassion Fatigue and Vicarious Traumatization

# THE COMPASSION FATIGUE WORKBOOK

## Françoise Mathieu

Routledge
Taylor & Francis Group
New York   London

This book is part of the Psychosocial Stress Series, edited by Charles R. Figley.

Routledge
Taylor & Francis Group
711 Third Avenue
New York, NY 10017

Routledge
Taylor & Francis Group
2 Park Square
Milton Park, Abington
Oxon OX14 4RN

© 2012 by Taylor & Francis Group, LLC
Routledge is an imprint of Taylor & Francis Group, an Informa business

Printed in the United States of America on acid-free paper
Version Date: 20111128

International Standard Book Number: 978-0-415-89790-7 (Paperback)

**Library of Congress Cataloging-in-Publication Data**

Mathieu, Françoise, 1969-The compassion fatigue workbook : creative tools for transforming compassion fatigue and vicarious traumatization / Françoise Mathieu. -- 1st ed.
    p. cm. -- (Routledge psychosocial stress series)
    Includes bibliographical references and index.
    ISBN 978-0-415-89790-7 (pbk. : alk. paper)
    1. Mental health personnel--Mental health. 2. Caregivers--Mental health. 3. Secondary traumatic stress. 4. Stress management. I. Title.

RC451.4.P79M38 2011
616.89'0230078--dc23

2011029457

**Visit the Taylor & Francis Web site at
http://www.taylorandfrancis.com**

**and the Routledge Web site at
http://www. Routledge.com**

This book is dedicated to my dear friend Robin Cameron, who co-wrote the early drafts of what became this workbook. Robin was also an integral part of the creation of the compassion fatigue workshops, nearly 10 years ago.

Robin, here's to our idea factories, our road trips, those thousands of envelopes we sealed, and the "everything" bagels we ate along the way. If it weren't for our 5-year journey together, none of this would be possible. Thank you!

# Contents

# Series Editor's Foreword

Linda's head was down as I joined her in my office for supervision. "I don't belong in the helping profession when I can't help myself," she said. It was our second supervisory session together at the trauma clinic at Florida State University in the early 1990s. This statement lingered for a few seconds until I responded in some reassuring way. By that time I had become far more savvy about the costs of caring, a topic I explored in depth in my 1995 book *Compassion Fatigue*, one of the many books that, like this one, is part of the Psychosocial Stress Series.

Fifteen years earlier I had experienced my first case of compassion fatigue. A man—let's call him "Chuck"—had just completed his doctoral studies and had taken a job as an assistant professor. He spent each week studying and teaching about marriages and families, and on the weekends he studied and made presentations to colleagues on the mental health challenges faced by combat veterans of the Vietnam War. Focusing on his work night and day became his life and ultimately cost him his marriage. But more about this case later.

It is with great pleasure that I welcome *The Compassion Fatigue Workbook*, by Françoise Mathieu, to the Routledge Psychosocial Stress Series. This is the 42nd book in the series, which includes dozens of books devoted to providing practical information for those exposed to considerable traumatic stress or, in this case, secondary traumatic stress.

Françoise is an Ontario-based practitioner who established Compassion Fatigue Solutions to offer consulting and training to helpers on topics related to self-care, wellness, burnout, and compassion fatigue. She is a certified mental health counselor with the Canadian Counseling and Psychotherapy Association and a compassion fatigue specialist with the Green Cross Academy of Traumatology. She has many years of experience as a crisis counselor working in a hospital emergency ward, in a university counseling service, and in other community mental health environments.

*The Compassion Fatigue Workbook* is a hands-on guide to self-care for practitioners. Our reviewers found her model of trauma and her strategies for self-care to be incredibly useful. Not only are they practical, but they also help clinicians to begin reviewing the costs of caring and making plans both for increasing compassion satisfaction and for rediscovering their joy for the work while simultaneously managing stress effectively and increasing resilience.

As Françoise notes in her introduction, this book emerged from years of experience in helping individuals and groups overcome work-related, toxic distress that had accumulated over many years. Françoise's writing is wonderful: she speaks from the heart, practitioner to practitioner, about the stressors and strains of human service work, particularly those that come from prolonged regular work with traumatized patients and clients.

It takes time to first recognize the toll of this field of work. Then it takes time to figure out what to do, and finally, it takes time to develop and implement a plan for self-care. In the 17 chapters of this book, readers will find practical advice laid out in a four-step process that helps readers take a thorough inventory of their life and life plans and develop their own personal path to wellness.

Returning to my first case of compassion fatigue: If Chuck had had the opportunity to read and use this book, he might have avoided the problems he faced in managing his emotional response to a regular dose of combat stories and to feeling the responsibility (compassion stress) of helping fellow veterans. It took more than a decade for Chuck to realize how bad—how debilitating— things had become. Chuck questioned his ability to study combat stress, just as my student therapist trainee Linda did in the trauma clinic 15 years later.

You see, I was "Chuck." I learned from my suffering, the hard way. Françoise Mathieu and I hope that you, as readers, will take advantage of what we and others have learned about the cost of caring.

**Charles R. Figley**
*Series Editor*
*Tulane University's Paul Henry Kurzweg*
*Distinguished Chair in Disaster Mental Health*
*New Orleans, Louisiana*

# Acknowledgments

## Influential Books

This workbook and my company's workshop series were inspired by Karen Saakvitne and Laurie Anne Pearlman's *Transforming the Pain* workbook, which was published in 1996 and was one of the very first books to propose concrete strategies for helping professionals in the workplace. About 10 years ago, my colleague Robin Cameron and I designed a one-day compassion fatigue workshop in our community, using Saakvitne and Pearlman's proposed template. We also read Charles Figley's two pioneering books *Compassion Fatigue: Coping With Secondary Traumatic Stress Disorder in Those Who Treat the Traumatized* and *Treating Compassion Fatigue*. Other pivotal readings included Pearlman and Saakvitne's *Trauma and the Therapist: Countertransference and Vicarious Traumatization in Psychotherapy With Incest Survivors*. I am indebted to these works for helping me shape this workbook.

This workbook was also guided and influenced by the quality work of Beth Hudnall Stamm, Anna Baranowsky, Eric Gentry, Peter Huggard, Laura van Dernoot Lipsky, Gabor Maté, Richard Harrison, and Patricia Fisher, to name but a few.

## Acknowledgments and Thanks

Some of the text in this book comes from the numerous blog posts I have written over the past 4 years. They can be found in their original form on my Web site: www.compassionfatigue.ca

I would like to thank Dr. Susan Tasker for her thoughtful feedback on this workbook and for proofreading the manual's early drafts. Thank you also to Babette Rothschild for her tremendous support, and Dr. Leslie Ross for her keen insights.

The field of compassion fatigue research is still in its infancy: the only way to make it move forward is to share ideas and explore concepts with colleagues. I have been very fortunate to find many people who were willing to share their thoughts, discuss ideas, and challenge some of my initial hunches as well. This learning community is invaluable to me. Thank you to Rebecca Brown, Lesley Carberrry and the whole team at Yukon Victim Services; Paula Chidwick, Naomi Giff MacKinnon for inviting me to the Northwest Territories and introducing me to a whole new world; Nancy Hogue, Margaret Lerhe, Leslie Maclean, Patrick Marshall, Stafford Murphy for giving us our first gigs; Rupa Patel, Richard Thomas, Diana Tikasz, Jack Truten, Tara Tucker, and Meaghan Welfare. Thank you to many others whom I have met along the way who have shared valuable feedback and insights. Thank you also to all the helping professionals who agreed to share their experiences, which are included as testimonials in this book.

Thank you to Wendy Craig for her unfailing support, and to Deb Thompson for helping me get started. A very special shout-out to my little family: NF, EF, and JRF. Sorry for all the trips away. I love you more than words can say. *Je vous aime plus gros que la lune.*

Finally, thank you to the thousands of workshop participants I have had the pleasure to meet during the last decade, who have so willingly shared their stories and sent questions and feedback.

## Author Disclaimer

This workbook is meant to target issues pertaining to how your work affects you. In working through the material you may experience powerful feelings and reactions. This book is not meant to be a substitute for psychological counseling or medical care. If you are feeling vulnerable at this time, it is best to combine working on this manual with psychotherapy. If you suspect that you are suffering from clinical depression or posttraumatic stress disorder, please seek the help of a mental health professional right away.

## Abbreviations

For simplicity's sake, I will sometimes refer to *compassion fatigue* as CF and *vicarious traumatization* as VT.

# Chapter 1

# Introduction

As part of Take Our Children to Work Day, I took my 14-year-old daughter to our busy clinic; she spent the day there with me, watching us work with patients and families. At the end of the day, over supper, I turned to her eagerly and said: "So, honey, what did you think?" She replied, "Well, I found out that you're a heck of a lot nicer at work than at home."

**—Community health nurse, Toronto, 2009**

In the coming year, your workplace budgets are probably going to get cut (yet again); your workload is likely going to increase but your salary isn't. You are going to be asked to do more with less and be given more paperwork and record-keeping tasks than you ever did before. Your face time with your clients, patients, and students will shrink, and you will be exposed to traumatic or difficult stories and be faced with moral and ethical dilemmas. You will have fewer referral resources and will work with some very cynical and burned-out colleagues. All of this will, in turn, impact your mood, energy levels, and ability to be present to your family and friends and may also interfere with the quality of your work and with your health.

The reality is that we work amid oceans of pain and there will always be more clients in need than we can possibly help. There are also significant flaws with the system, whether it be in health care, mental health, education, law enforcement, or the military. Many of us are also not equipped to deal with the traumatic nature of some of the work we do. It's tough out there for helping professionals. How can we make this work? Can we find ways to thrive in such a challenging environment?

## Were You Trained for This?

When I was completing my counseling degree in the mid-1990s, I took courses in three different countries; and not once, in any of these programs or with any of my clinical supervisors, did I hear the words *self-care, burnout,* or *compassion fatigue* mentioned. We were required to complete a one-credit course on ethical guidelines and best practice, which spoke of the importance of respecting client boundaries and confidentiality, but not once in any of these institutions were we told about the price we were about to pay, nor were we given tools to prevent it.

The second thing I quickly realized once I started working in the field is that I was very ill-equipped to deal with my clients' trauma, in spite of having a master's degree in counseling. I don't recall trauma ever being mentioned at university other than during one class on sexual abuse. So I learned on the job, sometimes scrambling to read as much as I could about my next client's issues right before he or she came to the session.

What about you? Back in college or university, did your program include a course on self-care, burnout, compassion fatigue, vicarious trauma, and moral distress? Do you feel that you received the proper training to do your work, or do you often feel that you are flying by the seat of your pants?

## Whose Responsibility Is It?

As a mental health counselor and former crisis worker, I have spent the last decade trying to find the best ways to assist other helping professionals to remain healthy while navigating the choppy waters of caregiving. My conclusion is that helpers need more resources to help them cope with the many challenges of their work. I also believe that our workplaces need to become more accountable in supporting us in our work by giving us access to proper debriefing, reducing our workload to realistic levels, and giving us more control over our schedules. But I also think that *we* as individuals need to take ownership of our own lives and our wellness. We cannot sit back and expect our organizations to take care of us.

There is a limit to what agencies can do with the limited funds they receive. I regularly meet very caring and worried managers and supervisors who are struggling to support their staff in this challenging environment. One manager once told me that she felt "like the jam in the sandwich: I'm being squeezed by all of my staff's demands and concerns; and on the other side I am being squeezed by senior management, the board and irate clients. I simply can't keep everyone happy." As a result, we are finding that managers are also feeling depleted and overtaxed. We all need to get involved in making these changes both at an organizational level and at a societal level.

My biggest challenge as a director is that I am trying to do the work of two people. When I moved into this position, I replaced a full-time counselor. I also replaced one of the pastors who had functioned as part-time overseer for the counseling center. My position as director should be a full-time position. It is impossible for me to successfully handle the responsibilities of both positions and to them both well.

**—Director of a women's counseling center**

When my colleague Robin Cameron and I designed our one-day compassion fatigue workshop for helping professionals nearly 10 years ago, we called it "Walking the Walk" because people in the helping field such as nurses, social workers, teachers, firefighters, clergy, and other health care professionals tend to be very good at helping other people but often have nothing left at the end of a long day for themselves. I believe that our industry needs to drastically improve its self-care if we are to remain effective and, better yet, thrive in today's challenging world. We have to walk the walk, not just talk the talk. This is what this workbook is all about.

---

### HOW TO USE THIS WORKBOOK

There is no wrong way to use this workbook. You can skip through and pick out the most useful tools, or you can work through it systematically chapter by chapter. To get the most benefit, I suggest setting aside some protected time each week to read and work through the exercises. This workbook will lead you through many experiential activities and offer concrete strategies that will hopefully help you make real changes in your personal and professional life. Please feel free to e-mail me with any comments or feedback: whp@cogeco.ca. My Web site also provides a wealth of additional resources and information: www.compassionfatigue.ca.

---

## First Things First

---

### GET A BUDDY/CREATE A SUPPORT SYSTEM

One of the best ways to use this workbook is to create a buddy system and work through the workbook together, one chapter per meeting. Find two or three friends or work colleagues and agree to meet weekly or speak to one another via e-mail, Skype, or phone. All of these exercises have been used in group settings during our workshops and are therefore designed to be extremely safe. However, I would strongly recommend that all group members read Chapter 5, "Low-Impact Debriefing," before meeting.

## SET ASIDE TIME

As your first commitment to yourself, I suggest that you set aside a minimum of 1 hour (and ideally 2 hours) per week to fully experience the benefits of this workbook. As the book progresses, you will be asked to make other commitments. Write them down, in ink, in your calendar—if you do not own a calendar or electronic day planner, please put this workbook down now and run to the nearest stationery store to get one! *Treat this time as respectfully as you would a promise to someone else you care for.*

## MAKE THIS WORKBOOK PART OF YOUR JOB

Ask if your workplace would be willing to help you pay for the cost of this workbook. More than three-quarters of the hundreds of helpers who have attended our live workshops had their attendance supported by their agency. In addition, you may ask your supervisor if you can work on the exercises during a protected professional development slot. Reserve a time when you will not be interrupted or bogged down by other work. You may need to play with the timing until you get it right—whatever works best for you is the right time.

## WRITE IT DOWN

Get yourself a journal, notebook, or binder—whatever you would prefer to use to document your personal process of working through this book. Many activities focus on just noticing, others require completing checklists and questionnaires, and finally, other activities will hone in on personal strategies for dealing with stress and compassion fatigue. You are likely to want to have your journal and workbook together somewhere in one place. Studies show that goals that are written down are accomplished more successfully than goals that are simply thought about. You have probably noticed this with people trying to lose weight or follow a budget. So write it down!

## *MAKING IT PERSONAL* HOMEWORK

This workbook offers many strategies for both home and work. For these strategies to actually work for you, you need to be willing to make real and lasting changes to the way you think and go about your life. Feeling overwhelmed didn't happen to you overnight, and it is not likely to improve just because you have this workbook and it sits on your desk day after day.

Be mindful that your inner critic may come up with lots of reasons why this won't work, why you won't be able to do this, why this isn't a good time, and most commonly: "But I already *know* all of this; I know how to have better self-care!" Helpers are better than anyone at "yes butting." In fact, we have "yes butted" our way into miserable self-care, poor health, and low moods. It is so easy to find a reason why we can't start an exercise program, eat better, or spend more time with friends. The goal of this workbook is to challenge you just slightly beyond your comfort zone but to keep all activities and change requests both reasonable and realistic.

Therefore, to maximize the benefits of this workbook, I recommend that you take the extra time to complete the homework after you have worked through each chapter.

---

**TAKE A RISK!**

In his book *The Resiliency Advantage,* Al Siebert wrote: "Your resiliency strengths come from self-motivated, self-managed efforts to develop resiliency skills. Some people who hear or read about ways to become more resilient mistakenly think that the power lies in the recommended method. They go through the steps in a detached way thinking the technique will make things better. Then when things don't turn out well, they blame the technique for not working. This is like tossing a can opener at a can of food and then blaming the can opener when the can doesn't open."[1] Don't blame the can opener: take a risk and follow the exercises in this workbook in earnest. If you make your own self-care a priority, you can make real changes to your life and mitigate the impact of compassion fatigue and vicarious traumatization.[2]

---

**HOW TO USE THIS WORKBOOK IN ORGANIZATIONAL SETTINGS**

This entire workbook can be used with your team or on your own. Many of the activities have been used in a large group workshop setting. Consider working on one chapter at a time with your colleagues and debriefing the exercises together during staff meetings.

## Endnotes

1. Siebert, A. (2005). *The resiliency advantage.* San Francisco: Berrett-Koehler, p. 13.
2. Thank you to Robin Cameron for her help with this section.

# Chapter 2

## Understanding the Cost of Caring

The expectation that we can be immersed in suffering and loss daily and not be touched by it is as unrealistic as expecting to be able to walk through water without getting wet. This sort of denial is no small matter. The way we deal with loss shapes our capacity to be present to life more than anything else. The way we protect ourselves from loss may be the way in which we distance ourselves from life. We burn out not because we don't care but because we don't grieve. We burn out because we've allowed our hearts to become so filled with loss that we have no room left to care.

**—Naomi Rachel Remen**
*Kitchen Table Wisdom,* p. 52

In this chapter you are invited to:

- Read the definitions of *compassion fatigue, vicarious traumatization,* and related terms.
- Read the narrative "A Story of CF and VT" with your journal/notebook close at hand. Note your thoughts and reactions to the story.
- Complete the writing exercise.
- Discuss your reactions to the narrative and to the exercise with your group or with a friend.

# A Normal Consequence of the Work

> I finally came to understand that my exposure to other people's trauma
> had changed me on a fundamental level. There had been an osmosis: I
> had absorbed and accumulated trauma to the point that it had become
> part of me, and my view of the world had changed.
>
> **—Laura van Dernoot Lipsky**
> *describing her own vicarious trauma in her book Trauma Stewardship:*
> *An Everyday Guide to Caring for Self While Caring for Others, p. 3*

The helping field has gradually begun to recognize that workers are profoundly
affected by the work they do, whether it is by direct exposure to traumatic events
(for example, working as a paramedic, firefighter, police officer, emergency hospital worker); secondary exposure (hearing clients talk about trauma they have
experienced, helping people who have just been victimized, working as child
protection workers); or the full gamut in between (such as working with clients
who are chronically in despair, witnessing people's inability to improve their very
difficult life circumstances, or feeling helpless in the face of poverty and emotional anguish).[1]

Our primary task as helping professionals is to meet the physical and/
or emotional needs of our clients and patients. This can be an immensely
rewarding experience, and the daily contact with clients is what keeps many
of us working in this field. It is a calling, a highly specialized type of work
that is unlike any other profession. However, this highly skilled and rewarding
profession can also look like this: increasingly stressful work environments,
heavy case loads and dwindling resources, cynicism and negativity from
co-workers, low job satisfaction, and for some, the risk of being physically
assaulted by clients.

*Compassion fatigue* (CF) refers to the profound emotional and physical
exhaustion that helping professionals and caregivers can develop over the
course of their career as helpers. It is a gradual erosion of all the things that
keep us connected to others in our caregiver role: our empathy, our hope,
and of course our compassion—not only for others but also for ourselves.
When we are suffering from compassion fatigue, we start seeing changes in
our personal and professional lives: we can become dispirited and increasingly bitter at work; we may contribute to a toxic work environment; we are
more prone to clinical errors; we may violate client boundaries and lose a
respectful stance towards our clients. We become short-tempered with our
loved ones and feel constant guilt or resentment at the never-ending demands
on our personal time.

CF has been described as "the cost of caring" for others in emotional pain.[2] It
can strike the most dedicated nurse, social worker, teacher, police officer, physician, and personal support worker alike. Ironically, helpers who are burned out,

worn down, fatigued, and traumatized tend to work more and work harder. As a result, they go further and further down a path that can lead to serious physical and mental health difficulties, such as depression, anxiety, substance abuse, chronic pain, other stress-related illnesses, and even suicide.

Compassion fatigue is an occupational hazard,[3] which means that almost every helper who cares about their patients/clients will eventually develop a certain amount of it, in varying degrees of severity. Charles Figley has called compassion fatigue a "disorder that affects those who do their work well."[4] The level of compassion fatigue that a helper experiences can ebb and flow from one day to the next, and even very healthy helpers with optimal work/life balance and self-care strategies can experience a higher than normal level of compassion fatigue when they are overloaded, are working with a lot of traumatic content, or find their case load suddenly heavy with clients who are all chronically in crisis. We do not develop compassion fatigue because we did something wrong—we develop it because we care, or because we *used* to care. Naomi Remen says it best, paraphrased from her quote above: We cannot walk through water without getting wet. We cannot do this work without being affected by it. (Well, that's not entirely accurate. We *can* do the work without caring, but everyone suffers—our colleagues, our clients, and our loved ones.)

*Vicarious traumatization* (VT) is a term that was coined by Laurie Anne Pearlman and Karen Saakvitne to describe the profound shift that workers experience in their world view when they work with clients who have experienced trauma. Helpers notice that their fundamental beliefs about the world are altered and possibly damaged by being repeatedly exposed to traumatic material. Vicarious trauma occurs when the stories we hear from our clients transfer onto us in a way where we too are traumatized by the images and details, even though we did not experience them ourselves. We then find it difficult to rid ourselves of the images and experiences they have shared with us. As Pearlman and Saakvitne explain, "It is not something clients do to us; it is a human consequence of knowing, caring, and facing the reality of trauma."[5]

VT is a cumulative process: we are not referring to the most difficult story you have ever heard; we are talking about the *thousands* of stories you don't even remember hearing. Where do those stories go at the end of your day? Have you ever found yourself struggling with intrusive images or nightmares that did not belong to you, but rather came from stories you had seen and heard at work? Have you found that your view of the world has changed because of the work that you do?

Some of us become increasingly numb to the pain and suffering of our clients; others feel profound sadness and anger at the unfairness of the world and many of us simply get overwhelmed. We were not provided with many tools to deal with this aspect of our work.

## A FAMILY PHYSICIAN GRAPPLES WITH VICARIOUS TRAUMA

*Vicarious trauma became real to me after about a month of working in a new practice. This was previously a "pain" practice with many of the patients being followed for chronic pain issues. As I got to know these people, I realized that their previous family doctors had never assessed them for trauma and abuse.*

*Soon every patient was disclosing significant stories of trauma to me. One day, I heard from six patients in a row about childhood neglect and abuse, sexual abuse by a private school teacher, violent partner abuse. These stories dominated the time I spent with patients. Some of these people had not disclosed to anyone ever before. This was overwhelming for me on a number of levels. First, I felt so sad. The stories of trauma are so unfair, particularly when a child is taken advantage of. Second, I was angry that these people had not been helped to deal with their issues and get some counseling. Third, I felt quite helpless, as I am not an expert in trauma issues, nor am I a counselor or a psychotherapist.*

*Over the ensuing days, I became preoccupied by the stories I had heard. I could not sleep at night. I also couldn't help but relive some of the horrors of the stories in my head. I did not want to share the trauma stories with others as I did not want to upset anyone else. The stories that I found so disturbing would be upsetting for others. I was paying less attention to my family. My children's shallow requests made me angry. I was irritable and very emotional. Twice, I walked into a meeting and broke into tears when someone me asked how I was.*

*Of course, this was classic vicarious trauma, which is a phenomenon I was aware of. But I still found it hard to recognize in myself. In retrospect, it is so obvious. But as one is experiencing the symptoms, there is a level of denial and hope that you can handle hearing all of these sad stories on your own.*

**—Dr. Rupa Patel, family physician**

## Aren't You Describing Burnout?

The simple answer is no. *Burnout* is a term that has been widely used to describe the physical and emotional exhaustion that workers can experience when they have low job satisfaction and feel powerless and overwhelmed at work. As Beth Stamm, a leader in the field, describes it, burnout refers to "the chronicity, acuity and complexity that is perceived to be beyond the capacity of the service provider."[6] This can most definitely affect many helping professionals in addition to compassion fatigue and vicarious trauma, but burnout does not necessarily mean that our view of the world has been damaged or that we have lost the ability to feel compassion for others.

Many nonhelping professionals suffer from burnout: in my counseling practice, I have worked with clients who were not in the helping field who felt severe

**TERMINOLOGY: A NEED FOR MORE CLARITY**

You have probably heard all sorts of terms that refer to the cost of caring, such as *secondary trauma, compassion stress, caregiver burnout, caregiver fatigue, bystander effect*, and several others. Nadine Najjar and colleagues recently did a review of all the research to date on compassion fatigue in cancer-care providers and they concluded that there is currently "an ambiguous definition of compassion fatigue that fails to adequately differentiate it from related constructs (e.g., burnout, secondary traumatic stress)."[7] Now, this is not really a problem for you as an individual helper, but it makes research difficult. Before we even carry out research on treating CF and VT, we need to be clear that we are all talking about the same thing. Beth Stamm says it best: "The controversy regarding secondary trauma is not its existence but what it should be called."[8] We are working on getting a set of working definitions we all agree on, but we're not there yet.

work-related burnout (e.g., someone working as an administrative assistant in a stressful real estate office, a factory worker, or an overtaxed call center worker). These individuals were frustrated and depleted by their work environment, but they did not find that their view of the world at large had been permanently transformed because of their work.

Many helpers are also at high risk for burnout due to working in difficult work environments with poor pay or little control over their schedule. Burnout can make us more vulnerable to CF and VT; an unsupportive work environment can create a fertile ground for cynicism and overwork. However, burnout itself can be fairly easily resolved: changing jobs can provide immediate relief to someone suffering from job-related burnout. This is not the case for CF and VT.

## Moral Distress

Moral distress is a concept that comes from the field of medical ethics. Gail Mitchell defines it as something that occurs "when policies or routines conflict with … beliefs about … patient care."[9] It happens when there is "incoherence between one's beliefs and values and one's actions, and possibly also outcome" as George Webster and Françoise Baylis have explained.[10] Simply put, moral distress occurs when we are told to do things that we fundamentally disagree with or to which we are morally opposed: having to discharge a patient prematurely, knowing full well that they have no support in the community and will relapse immediately; having to perform life-saving measures on a patient that had a DNR (do not resuscitate) order that is being overridden by family members; having to cut corners on client care because of the sheer volume of work; and the list goes on. Over time, moral distress can be a significant contributing factor to compassion fatigue.[11]

## MORAL DISTRESS IN THE HOSPITAL ENVIRONMENT

There was a chemotherapy drug that was not on the Provincial formulary but was being offered to a patient who was "well connected" and could afford to pay. As a result, the nurses in the outpatient clinic were expected to administer the drug to this patient, often with another patient with the same diagnosis sitting next to him/her. This created a great deal of moral distress for the nurses who felt it was inequitable—this became especially distressing when the patients started to talk to one another and then the patients who were not getting the treatment would ask the nurses why they were on a different treatment.

**— Testimonial from an oncology nurse**

Ethical dilemmas are what I respond to on a daily basis. They are not ordinary dilemmas but are situations where common sense is not helpful and what you usually do is not relevant. Ethical dilemmas are where there is no obvious right course of action, so there is a lot of moral distress, and in the end you are not left with more certainty but perhaps less. And this can be devastating and exhilarating—but over time it takes a toll, and if there is no renewal you begin to burn out. There is often conflict where deeply held views that clash are commonplace, and my job is to mediate, negotiate, and educate in these circumstances. Often people are left with moral residue. I feel like I have been party to something unethical. Detachment and resilience is important but sometimes hard to find. There is no peace in making tragic choices.

**—Dr. Paula Chidwick, ethicist**

When a physician orders a treatment that the nurse feels is too aggressive, and the patient has no hope of surviving or the quality of life will be greatly diminished, and the nurse feels the patient does not fully understand the implications of what he or she has agreed to, then the patient undergoes the treatment, does poorly, and the nurse is left to administer procedures that they believe are futile or will cause undue suffering. As one nurse describes, "and they gave him the treatment anyway, and he did not survive. ... It was very difficult to watch because you anticipated what the outcome was going to be at the outset, so to look after him day after day, it was hard, poking and prodding him, knowing that everything I did was not going to make a difference was extremely upsetting."

**—Testimonial from an oncology nurse**

# Primary and Secondary Trauma

*Primary trauma* is caused by a traumatic event that happens to you—you are directly exposed to the trauma. In the context of helping professionals, there are two kinds of primary trauma:

## *Primary Trauma From Your Personal Life*

This refers to trauma that you are carrying with you from your past (childhood abuse, having escaped a war, a traumatic loss in your personal life, surviving a motor vehicle accident, etc.). Research shows that more than 60% of helping professionals have a trauma history of their own, which may be why they chose this field of work (to make a difference, to give back, to share their learnings with others). That, in and of itself, is not a problem. The challenge arises when helpers go into the field without having done their own trauma work and are not aware of the ways in which their trauma history negatively impacts the work they do. It can also make us more vulnerable to developing vicarious trauma when bearing witness to our clients' pain and suffering.

## *Primary Trauma Caused by Work-Related Exposure*

This type of primary trauma exposure occurs in the line of duty: working as a firefighter, a search and rescue operator, being a first responder to an accident or a crime scene, being involved in a stakeout or negotiating a hostage taking, working in a war-torn country in unsafe conditions. What makes it *primary* is that it is happening *to* you. During this traumatic situation, you are potentially in harm's way and/or you are overwhelmed by the horror or terror of the situation.[12]

## *Secondary Trauma*

Secondary trauma is caused by a *secondary* exposure to trauma: you are not in actual danger; you are not at the scene of the traumatic event seeing firsthand the results of a shooting rampage or an accident. Instead, those stories are described to you verbally, in writing or through audio or video recordings. Secondary traumatic exposure can happen through counseling a client who is retelling a story of abuse, reading case files, debriefing a colleague or a client, sitting in court and hearing graphic testimonies, or watching a disturbing movie or traumatic news footage. In addition to the secondary trauma they are exposed to in the line of duty, many first responders such as firefighters and paramedics are at risk of developing primary trauma from their repeated exposure to traumatic events.

Both primary and secondary trauma exposure can lead to posttraumatic stress disorder (PTSD), an anxiety disorder that can develop after exposure to a traumatic event (or a series of traumatic events). It is characterized by re-experiencing (having nightmares or intrusive thoughts about the traumatic event), avoidance (e.g., avoiding triggers: not going in a car after an accident, avoiding churches if the trauma took place in a church), chronic tension and irritability, insomnia, difficulties with concentration and memory, and emotional numbing.[13]

Unfortunately, PTSD in helping professionals is often missed by family doctors or other health care professionals who have not received training in vicarious trauma or compassion fatigue. If you seek help from a health care practitioner for what you suspect is CF/VT related, make sure you check first whether they are familiar with these concepts. In fact, very few health care professionals have received even the most basic trauma training, and many trauma-related illnesses go undetected and untreated or get misdiagnosed and treated as depression or anxiety without a full context of the contributing factors.

## What Is the Difference Between Compassion Fatigue, Vicarious Trauma, Secondary Trauma, and Burnout?

These four terms are complementary and yet different from one another. While *compassion fatigue* refers to the profound emotional and physical erosion that takes place when helpers are unable to refuel and regenerate, the term *vicarious trauma* describes the transformation of our view of the world due to the cumulative exposure to traumatic images and stories. This is accompanied by intrusive thoughts and imagery and difficulty ridding ourselves of the traumatic experiences recounted by our clients. *Secondary traumatic stress* (STS) is the result of bearing witness to a traumatic event (or to a series of events), which can lead to PTSD-like symptoms (hearing a graphic account of abuse, debriefing first responders, etc.). I would argue that VT is the result of many STS events. *Burnout* has to do with the stress and frustration caused by the workplace: having poor pay, unrealistic demands, heavy workload, heavy shifts, poor management, and inadequate supervision; and as mentioned above, this can happen in any occupation.

---

**TRAUMA EXPOSURE RESPONSE: A NEW TERM TO DESCRIBE SECONDARY TRAUMA AND VT**

Laura van Dernoot Lipsky recently proposed a new term, *trauma exposure response*, which she defines as "a transformation that takes place within us as a result of exposure to the suffering of other living beings or the planet. This transformation can result from deliberate or inadvertent exposure, formal or informal contact, paid or volunteer work ... We are talking about ways in which the world looks and feels like a different place to you as a result of your doing your work."[14] Primary and secondary trauma and VT would fall under the umbrella of *trauma exposure response.*

## What Is the Difference Between CF and Depression?

Employees who considered most of their days to be quite a bit or extremely stressful were over three times more likely to suffer a major depressive episode, compared with those who reported low levels of general stress.

**—Canadian Mental Health Association[15]**

Dr. Richard Thomas, a clinical psychologist with many years of experience working with trauma survivors, explains the difference between CF and depression in the following way: "Depression is a recognizable mental illness defined in the *DSM-IV-TR*. Compassion fatigue … is more of an occupational hazard, for those in the helping professions—akin to an on-the-job type of safety hazard, if you will. My analogy: CF for helpers is roughly the emotional hazard equivalent to the physical hazards of fishermen working on an arctic fishing boat. Of course, if you change the circumstances to something healthier, the symptoms of the stress can mitigate and resolve with time. Chronic CF can certainly lead to depression, anxiety, addiction, or a host of other mental or physical illnesses, if it is not recognized and addressed effectively."[16] I would also add that having a history of depression and/or anxiety disorders can make a helping professional more vulnerable to compassion fatigue and vicarious trauma.

### YOU CAN SUFFER FROM VT WITHOUT SUFFERING FROM CF—AND VICE-VERSA

If I work as the assistant to a forensic psychologist and my task is to type the case files of violent sex offenders, I may be traumatized and deeply disturbed by the content of what I read. This may, in turn, affect my sex life, my feelings of safety for my children, or my ability to watch television (signs of vicarious trauma). I may still, however, have plenty of energy to talk to my friend who is going through a difficult time at home and I may not find that my work has caused me to feel deeply exhausted in my interactions with colleagues. But then again, I may experience all of the above.

If I work as a nurse in a long-term care facility helping patients who suffer from chronic illnesses, I may feel incredibly drained, fatigued, and unable to give any more at home or at work (signs of compassion fatigue); but I may not have become contaminated with graphic details of terrible things that people have experienced (car accidents, stories of sexual abuse, etc.). My world view about most things may still remain fairly intact.

---

### BEWARE: GOING TO A TRAUMA CONFERENCE COULD BE TRAUMATIC!

I was recently at a conference where the keynote speaker was introduced as an American expert in compassion fatigue. Her keynote speech consisted of two main parts: During the first part of her presentation, she showed us images of several first responders and told us about the ways in which they had committed suicide following a traumatic event (e.g., a firefighter who had helped survivors of the Oklahoma City bombing of the Federal Building, the first responder who rescued Baby Jessica many years ago). The speaker then said that these were examples of compassion fatigue. I was perplexed and waited to see where she was going with this.

She then talked about the importance of listening to our inner voice and told us about having recently met Aron Ralston, author of the book *Between a Rock and a Hard Place*. He is the American hiker who fell in a Utah canyon and had to amputate his arm to free himself back to safety. The keynote speaker then proceeded to tell us in graphic details the step-by-step process Ralston used to amputate his arm. The audience was groaning audibly and there was a wave of discomfort throughout the room. I sort of lost the message of her keynote at this point, and was just sitting there trying to fight a wave of nausea and feeling angry about this secondary traumatization.

I really don't think this speaker intended to traumatize the audience with her story. But two things occur frequently, even among specialists in the field: The first is the terminological confusion I mentioned earlier (the first responders in her story likely had PTSD, which led to their suicides. They may very well have had compassion fatigue, but the stories she told were not about CF—they were about primary trauma.) The second is that trauma specialists have become so desensitized to the graphic nature of the stories we've seen and heard that we sometimes inadvertently end up retraumatizing our audiences (for a strategy on how to prevent this, read Chapter 5, "Low-Impact Debriefing").

---

## Who Cares About the Difference Between These Terms?

The distinction between burnout, CF, VT, and primary and secondary trauma is important to provide you with the tools you need to clearly understand the factors that lead to you developing CF or VT: the more we know about the problem, the more we are able to develop strategies to prevent and modulate the impact of what we experience. It is also important to understand what we are bringing to the work we do in terms of our own primary trauma. But if you find that you're not sure "what you have," don't worry; I will explore this further in the coming chapters.

## Bringing This Closer to Home: *Your* CF/VT/Burnout and Primary Trauma

Helpers can experience compassion fatigue, vicarious trauma, burnout, and moral distress simultaneously. CF, VT, and moral distress are cumulative over time and evident in our personal and professional lives. They are also occupational hazards of working in the helping field. We will discuss this in the next sections of the workbook.

## My Story of Vicarious Trauma and Compassion Fatigue

### *Vicarious Trauma*

*I started working in this field when I was 21. My first experience was working as a volunteer in a hospital emergency ward in England as a "befriender." The task of the befriender was to comfort relatives whose loved ones had suffered an acute trauma or were very medically unstable. Family members were ushered into a special room to await news from medical staff. The befriender would offer to make a cup of tea or simply chat.*

*Understandably, the relatives in the family room were often highly distressed and some of them had also just been exposed to a traumatic event. Imagine that you go to a bar with your best friend, and he is stabbed in a knife fight, he gets rushed to hospital, and you end up waiting in the relatives' room. You will have a traumatic story to share with the first person who asks you how you are doing. If your child has been gravely injured in a car accident and you were driving the car but were miraculously unhurt, you will be sitting in that room waiting to hear life or death information about your child; and in this hospital, the befriender would be the person sitting there with you.*

*I had never done any counseling work before this—and needless to say, it was a pretty rapid and brutal introduction to the world of trauma (both physical and emotional). I remember feeling shocked and very shaken many evenings when returning home from work. I had no idea what was really happening to me except that I felt overwhelmed by what I had witnessed and also felt pretty incompetent at helping the people I met there. But I also loved the work—it felt like the right place for me, although that may seem contradictory. I found it deeply satisfying and unlike any other work I'd ever done.*

*I remember biking home in the evenings with my eyes as big as saucers, full of the stories I had heard, and then walking in the door and debriefing myself all over my scientist husband, who did not work in the field of trauma and who did not have training to deal with some of the stories I shared with him. I would slime him with all the gory details of my shift. One day, after telling him a particularly harrowing story involving children and loss of life, I saw how horrified he was and I started thinking about the contagious effect of my words.*

*Once I had debriefed from my shift, I would immediately turn on the TV to watch a show called* Casualty: Life in the ER. *I was so full of stories from the emergency ward that it seemed difficult to think about other things. Going out with friends, all I wanted to talk about were stories from the ER—what I had seen and heard. I also began finding that my view of the world was being tainted by my work: during car rides on the highway, I would have flashes of cars crashing, of drunk drivers smashing into us.*

These images are examples of vicarious trauma: being traumatized by the stories that we are bearing witness to during the course of our work.

There are many examples of ways in which exposure to difficult stories contaminates helpers: Many cancer care workers will tell you that for them, a headache is a sure sign of metastatic brain tumor. Many child protection workers confess to having a very difficult time hiring male babysitters for fear that they will molest their children, and that for them, any bruise on a child is a sign of abuse. The examples abound and are specific to the type of trauma you are exposed to during your work.

## A Loss of Innocence

*We fast forward to several years later—I now had two young children and was volunteering once a week in my son's kindergarten class. Initially, I enjoyed going into the classroom—it felt like a pure, simple way of reconnecting with young children and it also felt like a wonderful break from my work with soldiers and prison guards. Except that during my second day of volunteering, I noticed that one of my son's classmates had a bruise on his arm. Then I also noted that he did not seem to be wearing proper winter boots, and his lunch seemed meager and unhealthy. I started thinking of child protection scenarios and wondering what I should do. It felt as though I was starting to see potential child abuse everywhere I turned. Going to the public library, I would notice the disheveled mother who was being a bit short with her child, and I was taken away from enjoying my time at the library with my own children, always thinking to myself, "Should I intervene?"*

Think about your line of work. Has this happened to you? Different trades describe this loss of innocence in various ways: some people who work in prisons say that they have lost a sense of safety in their own homes because they work with offenders who have described to them, in great detail, home invasions and burglaries they have committed. When I worked in a university setting, I began seeing all female students as suffering from bulimia and all male students as pot-smokers who were failing on their exams. Of course, this was completely inaccurate, but my world view had become skewed by my repeated exposure to certain stories.

## Compassion Fatigue

*In the late 1990s I started working at a university counseling service as a crisis counselor. I worked there for 7 years (including a few baby breaks). When I initially considered working at the student counseling service, I hesitated at first, thinking that it wasn't going to be sufficiently challenging for me to deal with what I thought would be "small student issues" (relationship breakups, poor grades, and career dilemmas). I wanted to do emergency work—front-line, exciting stuff.*

*I couldn't have been more off base. I was the first person to hold the title of crisis counselor there and was exposed to a very high volume of clients and an incredible range of life issues—from complex sexual abuse histories that the clients had never disclosed before, to survivors of war traumas, to people coming for help in the middle of a full psychotic episode. Drastic province-wide budget cuts also meant that referral resources in the community were dwindling and I was often left dealing with highly complex problems with very few resources.*

*During my first few years as a crisis worker, I did not really notice that I was being profoundly affected by my work. I enjoyed what I did, although I often felt exhausted both physically and emotionally and frequently avoided social events. However, during the final 2 years at the counseling service, I started noticing the following behaviors:*

## Anger and Irritability

*I became extremely irritable with my colleagues. I resented the fact that they took lunch breaks while I was working nonstop, and I felt angry at the cheerful and positive demeanor of our support staff.*

Irritability with co-workers can be a symptom of compassion fatigue: you begin to feel resentful of colleagues and start to feel that you are doing all the work. Interestingly, research shows that individuals in the early stages of CF work harder rather than less. They can appear to be the most dedicated of staff (albeit humorless), take on extra responsibilities, and come to work early and leave late. Helpers with early CF often describe feeling overwhelmed with the workload, and say they have great difficulty setting limits and going home at the end of a shift. They often worry about their patients or clients and sometimes feel guilty about going home to a better environment than their clients' own situations.

## Avoidance of Meetings

*I started avoiding staff meetings as much as possible. This was largely because I felt frustrated hearing about more and more funding cuts and less resources for my clients, and also because I did not feel that I had time to stop and attend meetings. I felt that I should be seeing clients and trying to tackle my mounting waiting list.*

Unfortunately, missing staff meetings on a regular basis also means that we are losing opportunities to debrief with our colleagues. If numerous staff members stop attending meetings or peer supervision meetings because they are too busy with client work, staff morale can suffer.

## Predictability of Client Issues

*The clients I was working with were mostly 18- to 24-year-olds from similar back-grounds, and I started finding myself predicting ahead of time what my clients were going to talk about. This did not happen all the time, but often enough, I would find myself listening to a new client and I would think to myself: "Yup, I know what she's going to say next … I know where this is going."*

If you have ever worked with a highly homogenous client population, this may have happened to you as well. What is problematic about this behavior is that we stop asking important questions, which may cause us to miss key issues. Of course, with experience, we develop competence and confidence, and we become highly skilled at what we do. The problem, however, is that with confidence can also come complacency. Complacency can also lead us to make faulty assumptions about our clients—not asking a well-dressed professional whether she uses street drugs, assuming that a mother on social assistance is not taking proper care of her children, and others.

## Avoiding Difficult Topics With Clients

I have had helpers confess that they do not screen for suicide or homicide because they do not "have time to deal with it" or do not know how to respond to such concerns. Many health care professionals tend to avoid ask-ing trauma- or abuse-related questions for fear of opening a Pandora's box with the client. The truth is that many of us were not properly trained to deal with abuse and suicidal ideation.

## Feeling Discouraged About Lack of Referral Resources—Moral Distress

The reality for most of us is that we are doing more work with less and less resources. It can be very difficult to send someone away who is clearly in need but for whom we have nothing to offer. I was turning people away on a daily basis in my work as a crisis counselor, and that was probably the most difficult aspect of my job. It completely contradicted my reasons for choosing this line of work.

## Failure to Get a Life

*In my great wisdom, I thought it would be a good idea to volunteer after-hours at the local maximum security prison and volunteer to be on the board of directors of an eating disorder outreach program while working as a crisis counselor.*

This is not uncommon among helpers: First of all, our choice of career in the helping professions usually means that we are naturally inclined to help others and tend to be on the giving rather than the receiving end in our personal life as well as at work. Secondly, many of us volunteer on boards and help charitable organizations because we believe in giving back to our community. The problem is that, at some point, we have nothing left that is our own, which means that we cannot replenish ourselves.

## Fatigue and Exhaustion at the End of the Day

*I used to get home and be utterly exhausted, even though I had not necessarily worked a long shift, had slept 9 hours the previous night, and had not done any physical exercise. I was often puzzled when friends of mine, who were not in this field, would tell me about going to exercise class at night, after work. That seemed completely unimaginable for me.*

*My partner would come home and want to watch the news or talk about current events, and I would shut him down—I felt completely spent and only wanted to tell him about the most difficult stories I had heard, but I did not have much patience or tolerance for anything else. I also felt very easily overwhelmed by television—there was, I felt, far too much violence and sadness on TV. It did not feel like an escape for me.*

*I started becoming more and more interested in the phenomenon of CF and VT and began understanding that the exhaustion, irritability, and anger were being caused by my work but had to do with far more than a large caseload: I was being transformed and even sometimes damaged by the stories I was bearing witness to.*

### *MAKING IT PERSONAL* HOMEWORK: REFLECTION EXERCISE

In your journal/notebook, note your reactions to the narrative above: "My Story of VT and CF."

Can you relate to this? Do you agree/disagree? Is it bringing something up for you?

Consider taking some time to write down your own narrative of compassion fatigue, vicarious trauma, moral distress, and burnout. Providing you are not sharing graphic images or traumatic stories, consider sharing this narrative with a close friend or colleague.

If you are part of a group: at your first meeting/teleconference, share with one another how the narrative and the descriptions of CF and VT resonate with your own experiences. Note: It is highly recommended that everyone in the group read Chapter 5, "Low-Impact Debriefing," before your first meeting.

## WRITE YOUR OWN NARRATIVE

Take half an hour aside and write your own narrative of CF and VT. How would you tell the story of the work (or the caregiving) you have done? How did you start noticing the impact it was having on you?

Here are some questions to help you along:

1. Where do the stories go?
   What do you do at the end of a workday to put difficult stories from clients away before you go home?
2. Were you trained for this?
   Did your training offer you any education on self-care, compassion fatigue, vicarious trauma, or burnout? If it did, how up-to-date are you on those strategies? If it didn't, how much do you know about these concepts?
3. What are your particular vulnerabilities?

There are two things we know for sure about the field of helping: (a) a large percentage of helpers have experienced primary trauma at some point in their past, which may have led them to being attracted to the field in the first place; (b) personality types who are attracted to the field of helping are more likely to be highly attuned and to feel empathy toward others, which makes them good at their job *and* also more vulnerable to developing CF, VT, and burnout.

What are your vulnerabilities?

4. How do you protect yourself while doing this very challenging work?
5. Reread the story of your career as a helper.
   What have been the biggest challenges in your current job? Think broadly: client challenges, organizational challenges, interpersonal, societal, others? More specifically about your actual job, what have been or are the biggest challenges: your work schedule, colleagues, office layout, others?
   How did you come to realize that your work was having a significant impact on you and on your life?

Once you have written your story, take some time to review what you have written, and look for themes and patterns. What aspects of your CF/VT have to do with the nature of your work? What aspects have to do with your own history or family of origin? Can you see how the nature of your place of work may have impacted on your levels of CF and VT? Can you see how your own history or family of origin may have contributed to your levels of CF and VT?

If you feel comfortable doing so, consider discussing this with a colleague, friend, or counselor.

If you don't feel ready to do this, can you write down a few jots about your career path, what jobs you have had, and how they may have impacted you? For example:

1986 Kitchen helper—positive impact:           negative impact:
1990 Volunteer at women's shelter—positive impact:    negative impact:

If you are part of a group, discuss with one another how this chapter resonated with your own experiences of VT and/or CF.

## Endnotes

1. This section is adapted from an article entitled "Running on Empty," originally published in the Spring 2007 issue of *Rehab & Community Care Medicine.*
2. Figley, C.R. (Ed.). (1995). *Compassion fatigue: Coping with secondary traumatic stress disorder in those who treat the traumatized.* New York: Brunner/Mazel, p. 1.
3. Saakvitne, K.W., Pearlman, L.A., & the staff of the Traumatic Stress Institute. (1996). *Transforming the pain: A workbook on vicarious traumatization.* New York: W.W. Norton.
4. Figley, C.R. (1995). p. 5.
5. Saakvitne, K.W., & Pearlman, L.A., & Staff. (1996). p. 25.
6. Figley, C.R. (1995). p. 12.
7. Najjar, N., Davis, L.W., Beck-Coon, K., & Doebbeling, C.C. (2009). Compassion fatigue: A review of the research to date and relevance to cancer-care providers. *Journal of Health Psychology, 14*(2), 267.
8. Stamm, B.H. (Ed.). (1999). *Secondary traumatic stress: Self-care issues for clinicians, researchers, and educators* (2nd Edition). Lutherville: Sidran Press, p. 5.
9. Mitchell, G.J. (2001). Policy, procedure and routine: Matters of moral influence. *Nursing Science Quarterly, 14*(2), 110.
10. Webster, G.C., & Baylis, F.E. (2000). Moral residue. In S.B. Rubin & L. Zoloth (Eds.), *Margin of error: The ethics of mistakes in the practice of medicine* (p. 218). Haggerstown, MD: University Publishing Group.
11. "As discovered in research by Corley, 2002; Meltzer & Huckabay, 2004; and Severinsson, 2003, emotional exhaustion (a main component of burnout and compassion fatigue) has been significantly correlated with the frequency of moral distress." Leslie MacLean, personal communication, 2011.
12. Thank you to Diana Tikasz for this.
13. Butcher, J.N., Mineka, S., Hooley, J.M., Taylor, S., & Antony, M.M. (2007). *Abnormal psychology Canadian Edition.* Toronto: Pearson Canada.
14. van Dernoot Lipsky. (2009). p. 41.

15. Canadian Mental Health Association Web site, 2008. http://www.cmha.ca/bins/content_page.asp?cid=2-1841-1893-1898&lang=1 (accessed October 26, 2011).
16. Richard Thomas, PhD, clinical psychologist, personal communication, 2008.

# Chapter 3

## The ProQol: Professional Quality of Life Self-Test

Beth Stamm and Charles Figley have developed a self-test called the ProQol (Professional Quality of Life) that can be downloaded free of charge to assess one's own levels of secondary trauma, burnout, and compassion satisfaction.

In this chapter you are invited to:

- Learn more about compassion satisfaction
- assess your levels of CF/VT and Burnout with the Professional Quality of Life Self-Test
- Use the ProQol test results to map out your levels of CF, VT and burnout

### What Is Compassion Satisfaction?

Beth Stamm describes compassion satisfaction as "the pleasure you derive from being able to do your work well."[1] Stamm considers compassion fatigue (CF) to be the result of both burnout and secondary trauma (keeping in mind the terminological debate discussed in Chapter 2), so your test scores for both categories provide a picture of your CF, in her opinion. I'm not sure I completely agree, as I have seen individuals who work in highly supportive work environments with nontraumatized clients still develop compassion fatigue, but no matter. This test is a great tool and one that has been used throughout the world to collect reliable data on the cost of caring. It is being reproduced here with permission.

I would now like to invite you to take a few minutes to take the test (reproduced on the following pages in Figure 3.1). To download this test, go to http://www.proqol.org/ProQol_Test.html. Beth Stamm would also greatly appreciate it if you are willing to submit your test results to her, because she is compiling

**PROFESSIONAL QUALITY OF LIFE SCALE (PROQOL)**

COMPASSION SATISFACTION AND COMPASSION FATIGUE
(PROQOL) VERSION 5 (2009)

When you *[help]* people you have direct contact with their lives. As you may have found, your compassion for those you *[help]* can affect you in positive and negative ways. Below are some questions about your experiences, both positive and negative, as a *[helper]*. Consider each of the following questions about you and your current work situation. Select the number that honestly reflects how frequently you experienced these things in the *last 30 days*.

| 1=Never | 2=Rarely | 3=Sometimes | 4=Often | 5=Very Often |
|---|---|---|---|---|

_____ 1. I am happy.

_____ 2. I am preoccupied with more than one person I *[help]*.

_____ 3. I get satisfaction from being able to *[help]* people.

_____ 4. I feel connected to others.

_____ 5. I jump or am startled by unexpected sounds.

_____ 6. I feel invigorated after working with those I *[help]*.

_____ 7. I find it difficult to separate my personal life from my life as a *[helper]*.

_____ 8. I am not as productive at work because I am losing sleep over traumatic experiences of a person I *[help]*.

_____ 9. I think that I might have been affected by the traumatic stress of those I *[help]*.

_____ 10. I feel trapped by my job as a *[helper]*.

_____ 11. Because of my *[helping]*, I have felt "on edge" about various things.

_____ 12. I like my work as a *[helper]*.

_____ 13. I feel depressed because of the traumatic experiences of the people I *[help]*.

_____ 14. I feel as though I am experiencing the trauma of someone I have *[helped]*.

_____ 15. I have beliefs that sustain me.

_____ 16. I am pleased with how I am able to keep up with *[helping]* techniques and protocols.

_____ 17. I am the person I always wanted to be.

_____ 18. My work makes me feel satisfied.

_____ 19. I feel worn out because of my work as a *[helper]*.

_____ 20. I have happy thoughts and feelings about those I *[help]* and how I could help them.

_____ 21. I feel overwhelmed because my case [work] load seems endless.

_____ 22. I believe I can make a difference through my work.

_____ 23. I avoid certain activities or situations because they remind me of frightening experiences of the people I *[help]*.

_____ 24. I am proud of what I can do to *[help]*.

_____ 25. As a result of my *[helping]*, I have intrusive, frightening thoughts.

_____ 26. I feel "bogged down" by the system.

_____ 27. I have thoughts that I am a "success" as a *[helper]*.

_____ 28. I can't recall important parts of my work with trauma victims.

_____ 29. I am a very caring person.

_____ 30. I am happy that I chose to do this work.

**Figure 3.1(a)** Stamm, B.H. (2010). The ProQOL (*Professional Quality of Life Scale: Compassion Satisfaction and Compassion Fatigue*). Pocatello, ID: ProQOL.org. Retrieved May 2011 from www.proqol.org **(continued)**

## YOUR SCORES ON THE PROQOL: PROFESSIONAL QUALITY OF LIFE SCREENING

Based on your responses, place your personal scores below. If you have any concerns, you should discuss them with a physical or mental health care professional.

### Compassion Satisfaction _____

Compassion satisfaction is about the pleasure you derive from being able to do your work well. For example, you may feel like it is a pleasure to help others through your work. You may feel positively about your colleagues or your ability to contribute to the work setting or even the greater good of society. Higher scores on this scale represent a greater satisfaction related to your ability to be an effective caregiver in your job.

The average score is 50 (SD 10; alpha scale reliability .88). About 25% of people score higher than 57 and about 25% of people score below 43. If you are in the higher range, you probably derive a good deal of professional satisfaction from your position. If your scores are below 40, you may either find problems with your job, or there may be some other reason—for example, you might derive your satisfaction from activities other than your job.

### Burnout_____

Most people have an intuitive idea of what burnout is. From the research perspective, burnout is one of the elements of Compassion Fatigue (CF). It is associated with feelings of hopelessness and difficulties in dealing with work or in doing your job effectively. These negative feelings usually have a gradual onset. They can reflect the feeling that your efforts make no difference, or they can be associated with a very high workload or a non-supportive work environment. Higher scores on this scale mean that you are at higher risk for burnout.

The average score on the burnout scale is 50 (SD 10; alpha scale reliability .75). About 25% of people score above 57 and about 25% of people score below 43. If your score is below 18, this probably reflects positive feelings about your ability to be effective in your work. If you score above 57 you may wish to think about what at work makes you feel like you are not effective in your position. Your score may reflect your mood; perhaps you were having a "bad day" or are in need of some time off. If the high score persists or if it is reflective of other worries, it may be a cause for concern.

### Secondary Traumatic Stress_____

The second component of Compassion Fatigue (CF) is secondary traumatic stress (STS). It is about your work related, secondary exposure to extremely or traumatically stressful events. Developing problems due to exposure to other's trauma is somewhat rare but does happen to many people who care for those who have experienced extremely or traumatically stressful events. For example, you may repeatedly hear stories about the traumatic things that happen to other people, commonly called Vicarious Traumatization. If your work puts you directly in the path of danger, for example, field work in a war or area of civil violence, this is not secondary exposure; your exposure is primary. However, if you are exposed to others' traumatic events as a result of your work, for example, as a therapist or an emergency worker, this is secondary exposure. The symptoms of STS are usually rapid in onset and associated with a particular event. They may include being afraid, having difficulty sleeping, having images of the upsetting event pop into your mind, or avoiding things that remind you of the event.

The average score on this scale is 50 (SD 10; alpha scale reliability .81). About 25% of people score below 43 and about 25% of people score above 57. If your score is above 57, you may want to take some time to think about what at work may be frightening to you or if there is some other reason for the elevated score. While higher scores do not mean that you do have a problem, they are an indication that you may want to examine how you feel about your work and your work environment. You may wish to discuss this with your supervisor, a colleague, or a health care professional.

**Figure 3.1(b)   Stamm, B.H. (2010). The ProQOL (*Professional Quality of Life Scale: Compassion Satisfaction and Compassion Fatigue*). Pocatello, ID: ProQOL.org. Retrieved May 2011 from www.proqol.org (continued)**

## WHAT IS MY SCORE AND WHAT DOES IT MEAN?

In this section, you will score your test and then you can compare your score to the interpretation below.

To find your score on **each section,** total the questions listed on the left in each section and then find your score in the table on the right of the section.

### Compassion Satisfaction Scale:

3. _____
6. _____
12. _____
16. _____
18. _____
20. _____
22. _____
24. _____
27. _____
30. _____
**Total:** _____

| The sum of my Compassion Satisfaction questions | So My Score Equals | My Level of Compassion |
|---|---|---|
| 22 or less | 43 or less | Low |
| Between 23 and 41 | Around 50 | Average |
| 42 or more | 57 or more | High |

### Burnout Scale:

*1. _____ = _____
*4. _____ = _____
8. _____
10. _____
*15. _____ = _____
*17. _____ = _____
19. _____
21. _____
26. _____
*29. _____ = _____

| The sum of my Burnout Questions | So My Score Equals | My Level of Burnout |
|---|---|---|
| 22 or less | 43 or less | Low |
| Between 23 and 41 | Around 50 | Average |
| 42 or more | 57 or more | High |

Reverse the scores for those that are starred.
0=0, 1=5, 2=4, 3=3, 4=2, 5=1
**Total:** _____

### Secondary Trauma Scale:

2. _____
5. _____
7. _____
9. _____
11. _____
13. _____
14. _____
23. _____
25. _____
28. _____
**Total:** _____

| The sum of my Secondary Traumatic Stress questions | So My Score Equals | My Level of Secondary Traumatic Stress |
|---|---|---|
| 22 or less | 43 or less | Low |
| Between 23 and 41 | Around 50 | Average |
| 42 or more | 57 or more | High |

**Figure 3.1(c)** (continued) Stamm, B.H. (2010). The ProQOL (*Professional Quality of Life Scale: Compassion Satisfaction and Compassion Fatigue*). Pocatello, ID: ProQOL.org. Retrieved May 2011 from www.proqol.org

data on the effectiveness of the test. Please visit her Web site for more information: www.proqol.org.

## ProQol Self-Test Results

What are your thoughts/reactions to your results?

> Compassion Satisfaction
> Burnout
> Secondary Trauma

After you have read the definitions in the previous chapter, and with your ProQol results in hand, take a look at the following graphs, which offer a visual guide to CF, secondary trauma, burnout, and primary trauma.

Many of us will have overlap and will simultaneously experience burnout, CF, and secondary and primary trauma. However, depending on the type of work you do, you may not have a great deal of exposure to trauma.

If I love my job and have a very supportive work environment, but have a lot of trauma exposure *and* have experienced primary trauma in my life and job, I might highlight the circles as in Figure 3.2.

If I have a lot of burnout (due to poor working conditions, an unsupportive manager, etc.) and compassion fatigue, but no exposure to trauma in my work life or in my past, I might highlight those as in Figure 3.3.

Many of us will end up right in the middle, with quite a bit of all four (Figure 3.4).

In the graph in Figure 3.5, color in where you see yourself at the moment. Is there a lot of overlap, or are you concentrated in one or two areas only?

The better you understand the source of the stressors, the sooner you will be able to develop an intervention plan for yourself. We will discuss this in more detail in the chapters to come.

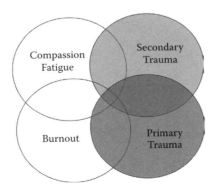

**Figure 3.2**

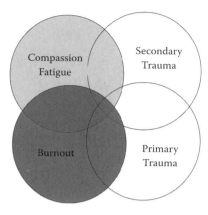

**Figure 3.3**

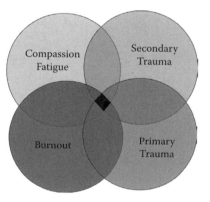

**Figure 3.4**

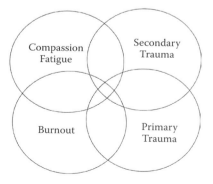

**Figure 3.5**

**RECOMMENDED READING:** *TRAUMA STEWARDSHIP*—A MUST FOR ANYONE DOING TRAUMA WORK

Laura van Dernoot Lipsky's wonderful book *Trauma Stewardship*[2] fills a real void in the field of vicarious trauma resources. Laurie Anne Pearlman and her colleagues gave us the cornerstone books *Transforming the Pain* and *Trauma and the Therapist*, but we were in dire need for a book that provides concrete steps to help us navigate the challenging field of trauma work. Lipsky guides us through new ways to navigate trauma exposure and implement lasting changes in our daily lives.

## Endnotes

1. Stamm, B.H. (2005). *The ProQOL manual: The professional quality of life scale: Compassion satisfaction, burnout & compassion fatigue/secondary traumatic scale.* Baltimore: Sidran Press, p. 12.
2. van Dernoot Lipsky, L., & Burk, C. (2009). *Trauma stewardship: An everyday guide to caring for self while caring for others.* San Francisco: Berrett-Koehler.

# Chapter 4

# How Many Helpers Develop Compassion Fatigue and Vicarious Trauma?

More than 40% of nurses surveyed said they would not feel comfortable having a family member cared for in the facility in which they work. Over 54% of respondents would not recommend their profession to their children or friends.

**—American Nursing Association Staffing Survey, 2001**

A recent study among chaplains in the Canadian military found that 52% of chaplains were at medium to high risk for anxiety or depressive disorders.

**—Canadian Press, May 16, 2010**

In this chapter you are invited to:

- Read through some of the statistics on the incidence rates of compassion fatigue (CF) and vicarious trauma (VT)
- Do a bit of research (see homework)
- Have a conversation in your workplace about the cost of caring

The field of compassion fatigue and vicarious trauma research is growing very rapidly. In fact, there are currently more master's and PhD theses being written on the topic than ever before. This will lead to a wonderful explosion of research in the coming years. In the meantime, the data collected during the past 15 years are highly consistent: many helpers across the various helping fields (teachers, physicians, nurses, social workers, animal shelter workers, paramedics, psychologists, shelter workers, prison therapists, judges, police officers, chaplains, etc.) are showing clear signs of compassion fatigue and vicarious trauma.

Most studies come to the same conclusions: Compassion fatigue affects the most caring,[1] and the more trauma you have on your caseload, the more likely you are to develop vicarious trauma.[2] In addition, having a trauma history of your own makes you more vulnerable to developing CF and VT.

Depending on the studies, between 40% and 85% of helping professionals were found to have compassion fatigue and/or high rates of traumatic symptoms.[3] For example, a recent study carried out among Florida hospice nurses found that 79% of them had moderate to high rates of compassion fatigue, and 83% of those who did not have debriefing or other support after a patient's death had symptoms of CF.[4] Several studies of child welfare workers found that nearly half of them reported traumatic stress symptoms in the severe range.[5] Similar findings have been reported among other helping professionals such as child protection workers, law enforcement officers, counselors, and prison guards in Canada, the United States, Australia, New Zealand, and other countries around the world.[6]

## Threats and Assault

Research has also shown that some helpers such as nurses and social workers are regularly threatened by patients or their family members. One study found that 57% of social workers had been threatened and 16% had been physically assaulted.[7] Another study found that 90% of trauma workers had been verbally abused and more than 40% had been physically assaulted at work.[8] Nurses report regular workplace violence and were found "more likely to experience on the job violence than all other professions."[9] A recent survey of nurses found that one-third of all nurses had been physically assaulted in the past year. In many of these studies, there was a strong correlation between having been assaulted and developing compassion fatigue.

## Some Canadian Data

Statistics Canada recently published their first-ever National Survey of the Work and Health of Nurses in 2005, which found that "close to one-fifth of nurses reported that their mental health had made their workload difficult to handle during the previous month."[23] In the year before the survey, more than half of the nurses surveyed had taken time off work because of a physical illness, and 10% had been away for mental health reasons. Eight out of 10 nurses accessed their EAP (employee assistance program), which is more than twice as high as EAP use by the rest of the total employed population.

A study of cancer-care workers in Ontario also found high levels of burnout and stress among oncology workers and discovered that a significant number of them were considering leaving the field: 50% of physicians and one-third of other cancer-care professionals had high levels of emotional exhaustion and low levels of personal accomplishment.[10]

## A SAMPLING OF CF/VT IN OTHER PROFESSIONS

### DOMESTIC VIOLENCE LAWYERS

A survey of domestic violence lawyers found significantly higher levels of secondary traumatic stress and burnout compared with mental health providers and social service workers.[11]

### JUNIOR DOCTORS

In a 2009 study by the Australian Medical Association, 54% of junior doctors (residents) met the criteria for CF, 69% met the criteria for burnout, and 71% had lower than average levels of job satisfaction.[12]

### SURGEONS

A recent study of American surgeons indicated that in the past year, surgeons thought about suicide 1.5–3 times more than the general population. Only 26% of those with suicidal ideation (SI) had sought help for their suicidal symptoms: "Although 1 of 16 surgeons reported SI in the previous year, few sought psychiatric or psychological help. Recent SI among surgeons was strongly related to symptoms of depression and a surgeon's degree of burnout."[13]

### CLERGY

In a survey of more than 2,500 U.S. clergy members, "76% of them were overweight or obese, compared to 61% of the general population."[14] A study of another clergy group reported that 40% of them "experienced mild to severe burnout." A third survey found that 74% of clergy felt there were too many demands on their time.[14]

### IMMIGRATION JUDGES

U.S. immigration judges were found to have some of the highest levels of burnout and secondary trauma: "A study published last year based on surveys of 96 U.S. immigration judges found their burnout level to be higher than that of hospital physicians and prison wardens. The study, which appeared in the *Georgetown Immigration Law Journal*, noted that judges expressed frustration over being 'extremely overburdened.' … The judges, who also completed psychological testing as part of their surveys, showed signs of 'compassion fatigue' and 'secondary traumatic stress' stemming from working with trauma victims such as immigrants who are seeking asylum in the United States because of violence or persecution in their homelands."[15]

**LAW ENFORCEMENT: WHO IS WILLING TO SEEK HELP?**

Interestingly, one study found that mental health professionals were far more likely to seek personal counseling than law enforcement professionals: 59% of mental health professionals were willing to seek help, versus 15% of law enforcement professionals.[16]

## Risk Factors

Researchers have identified vulnerability factors that increase the likelihood of a helper developing more severe levels of CF and VT: A history of childhood trauma, coping style, difficult life circumstances, working conditions, and as Maryann Abendroth terms it, "excessive empathy leading to blurred professional boundaries."[17] We will discuss these risk factors in more detail in Chapter 7.

## The Challenge: Getting Stakeholders to Acknowledge That CF Exists

### Law Enforcement and EMTs

Some of the toughest audiences my associates and I have come across in the past few years have been in law enforcement and emergency personnel (paramedics, firefighters). There still seems to be an "if you can't stand the heat, get out of the kitchen" mentality among many first responders that does not allow for an open dialogue about CF and VT among peers. I have met many rookie police officers in the RCMP (Royal Canadian Mounted Police) whose first postings were in very remote northern communities, some with a staggering rate of abuse and

**A RESOURCE FOR LAW ENFORCEMENT PERSONNEL**

I was given a great booklet by an RCMP officer in the Yukon a few months ago who said that it is being made available to all Yukon-based RCMP members and that he had found it extremely useful:

Gilmartin, K.M. (2002). *Emotional survival for law enforcement: A guide for officers and their families*. Tucson: E-S Press.

The author is a former police officer and behavioral scientist. This is a nicely written, down-to-earth resource designed to provide new recruits with the tools to protect themselves from posttraumatic stress disorder (PTSD) and occupational stress. The book can be ordered online: http://emotionalsurvival.com/

violence. These rookies were practically air-dropped in these villages with little or no training on how to deal with traumatized individuals, let alone how to deal with their own trauma. This is changing, but at a snail's pace.

### A Changing Landscape, for the Better

Nearly 10 years ago, when we ran our first compassion fatigue workshop, about half of the audience said that they had to pay their own way and/or take a sick day from work to attend. Many said that they did not want their manager to know they were attending a workshop on burnout and compassion fatigue because they feared that they would end up being labeled as having something wrong with them when they returned to the workplace.

Thankfully, in my experience, this attitude has improved since then, in some agencies at least. During the past decade, I have seen a very encouraging shift among agencies and funders in their acknowledgment of CF and VT as realities in the workplace. I have worked with several forward-thinking agencies that put a great deal of time and funding toward implementing comprehensive CF training among staff, with monthly check-ins and train-the-trainer courses to raise awareness and educate their employees and managers. There is now a recognition in many (though not all) helping fields that CF and VT present a clear occupational health and safety hazard to staff. The sheer cost of long-term disability and sick leave is bringing these health problems to the forefront, as are the staggering rates of workplace conflict and difficulty retaining new staff members. These concerns are highlighted in Linda Duxbury's recent report on role overload.

## The Duxbury Report on Role Overload

Linda Duxbury recently carried out a study of role overload in health care. She defines *role overload* as having too many competing demands and too many roles (too much work, not enough time). With ongoing budgetary restrictions and staffing reductions, juggling multiple roles is a common reality in the helping professions. Duxbury found that almost three out of five health care workers were suffering from role overload.[18]

### High Turnover and High Absenteeism

Duxbury also found that one in four employees was planning on leaving their job at the hospital. What's interesting about this finding, however, is that they wanted to leave not for higher pay elsewhere but rather because they wanted a job where they had "greater control over work hours and more respect." One in three staff members missed work "due to emotional and physical fatigue."[19]

## Worrisome Rates of Poor Mental and Physical Health

Duxbury found that health care workers were in poorer physical and mental health than staff surveyed in other sectors of the population. In health care, "59% report high levels of stress, 36% report high levels of depressed mood and one in five are in poor physical health."[20] Similar data have been found in the United States and other countries as well.[21,22]

## Getting Help

Another obstacle we still face has to do with Employee Assistance Programs (EAPs). The quality of EAPs varies widely: some EAPs hire well-qualified mental health counselors and offer a reasonable number of sessions to clients, but some do not. About 3 years ago, I asked several hundred staff members who worked in a large agency to call their EAP to inquire whether their counselors had received CF training. The answer at the time was a unanimous no, that it was beyond the scope of the EAP's mandate. Since then, I have seen some evidence that this is slowly changing: some EAPs are beginning to incorporate concepts of compassion fatigue and vicarious trauma in their stress management workshops, but still not enough EAP counselors have training in CF, and therefore few of them are well equipped to offer adequate treatment to helpers.

## Human Resource Initiatives: Do Wellness Workshops Work?

Human resources staff (even in health care agencies) are not always aware of concepts related to CF. An informal survey of all the agencies I have visited suggest that the "stress busters 101" sessions offered by EAP or HR do not meet the complex needs of helpers in the field. In addition, there are still obstacles to participating in a CF workshop: How safe is it to attend a work-sponsored workshop on this topic? Not all helping professionals will feel comfortable discussing their symptoms of CF and work-related dissatisfaction with their colleagues. In-house CF workshops are valuable but have their limits; participants may take a lot in but may not participate outwardly very much.

## Keeping it Meaningful

How many times have you attended a workshop, listened to a radio show, or read an inspirational book, only to forget all about it only minutes or days later? We know that our attention span as learners is short; therefore our ability to retain a full day's worth of information on any topic will be limited. Most of us need to hammer out a clear commitment to concrete change or else a workshop's lessons will dissipate rather quickly.

**YOUR SUPPORT STAFF CAN BE AFFECTED, TOO**

Receptionists, custodians, court reporters, administrative assistants—all are too often the invisible recipients of a great deal of traumatic material. As staff members, we often treat them like the local bartender, unloading the stresses and complaints of our days on them, as we lean against the counter of the reception desk. They are often the first point of contact for irate callers and clients walking into our busy clinics, or for angry parents phoning the school.

CF and VT are in the air we breathe; it's in the ventilation system of the office, so to speak. Being a receptionist for your agency is nothing like working the desk in a real estate office. Support staff need and deserve our support. They also deserve to receive basic training on the impact of CF and VT on their own world view and well-being.

**RECOMMENDED READING**

To read more on the concepts discussed in this chapter (see also the research papers in the endnotes):

Figley, C. R. (Ed.). (1995). *Compassion fatigue: Coping with secondary traumatic stress disorder in those who treat the traumatized.* New York: Brunner/Mazel.

Figley, C. R. (Ed.). (2002). *Treating compassion fatigue.* New York: Brunner/Routledge.

Pearlman, L. A., & Saakvitne, K. W. (1995). *Trauma and the therapist: Countertransference and vicarious traumatization in psychotherapy with incest survivors.* New York: W.W. Norton.

Stamm, B. H. (Ed.). (1999). *Secondary traumatic stress: Self-care issues for clinicians, researchers, and educators* (2nd Edition). Lutherville, MD: Sidran Press.

**_MAKING IT PERSONAL_ HOMEWORK**

*Do a bit of research:* If you don't find your profession in the data above, take a few minutes and do a Google search specific to your trade. You may find some interesting research findings, or you may find that very little research has been done on your specific group.

*Have a conversation* about the data presented in this chapter with your colleagues. Do these numbers surprise them?

## Endnotes

1. Figley, C.R. (Ed.). (1995). *Compassion fatigue: Coping with secondary traumatic stress disorder in those who treat the traumatized.* New York: Brunner/Mazel, p.1.

2. Figley, C.R. (Ed.). (1995); Stamm, B.H. (Ed.). (1999). *Secondary traumatic stress: Self-care issues for clinicians, researchers, and educators* (2nd Edition). Lutherville, MD: Sidran Press; and many others since.

3. For a comprehensive compilation of research to date in the nursing field, read Tatano Beck, C. (2011). Secondary traumatic stress in nurses: A systematic review. *Archives of Psychiatric Nursing, 25*(1) (February), 1–10.

4. Abendroth, M., & Flannery, J. (2006). Predicting the risk of compassion fatigue: A study of hospice nurses. *Journal of Hospice and Palliative Nursing, 8*(6), 346–356.

5. Conrad, D., & Kellar-Guenther, Y. (2006). Compassion fatigue, burnout, and compassion satisfaction among Colorado child protection workers. *Child Abuse and Neglect, 30*(10) 1071–1080.

6. Adams, R.E., Boscarino, J.A., & Figley, C.R. (2006). Compassion fatigue and psychological distress among social workers: A validation study. *American Journal of Orthopsychiatry, 76*(1), 103–108.

7. Bell, H., Kulkarni, S., & Dalton, L. (2003). Organizational prevention of vicarious trauma. *Families in Society, 84*(4), 463–470.

8. Crabbe, J.M., Bowley, D.M.G., Boffard, K.D., Alexander, D.A., & Klein, S. (2004). Are health professionals getting caught in the crossfire? The personal implications of caring for trauma victims. *Emerg Med J, 21*, 568–572.

9. Ontario Nursing Association Web site, 2006.

10. Grunfeld, E. (2000, July 25). Cancer care workers in Ontario: Prevalence of burnout, job stress and job satisfaction. *CMAJ, 163*(2), 166–169.

11. Levin, A.P., & Greisberg, S. (2003). Vicarious trauma in attorneys. *Pace L. Rev., 24*(1), 245–246.

12. Markwell, A., & Wainer, Z. (2009). Doctors' health. *MJA, 191*(8), 19.

13. Shanafelt, T.D., Balch, C.M., Dyrbye, L., Bechamps, G., Russell, T., Satele, D. et al. (2011). Suicidal ideation among American surgeons. *Arch Surg, 146*(1), 54–62.

14. Ferguson, S. (2007). Clergy compassion fatigue. *Family Therapy Mag,* March-April.

15. Curtis, L. (2010). Case backlog postponing deportations proceedings increase 26 percent, but immigration judges swamped. *Las Vegas Review Journal,* May 30.

16. Bell, H., Kulkarni, S., & Dalton, L. (2003). Organizational prevention of vicarious trauma. *Families in Society, 84*(4), 463–470.

17. Abendroth, M., & Flannery, J. (2006), p. 352.

18. Duxbury, L., Higgins, C., & Lyons, S. (2009). The etiology and reduction of role overload in Canada's health care sector. Funded by a grant from the Workplace, Safety and Insurance Board. Available online.

19. Duxbury, L., Higgins, C., & Lyons, S. (2009), p. 89.

20. Duxbury, L., Higgins, C., & Lyons, S. (2009), p. 56.

21. ANA Staffing Survey. (Feb. 6, 2001). See www.nursingworld.org/staffing/ for details.

22. Crabbe, J.M., et al. (2004).

23. Statistics Canada. (2006). National Survey of the Work and Health of Nurses. Released December 11, 2006. www.statcan.gc.ca (accessed October 26, 2011).

# Chapter 5

# Low-Impact Debriefing: How to Stop Sliming Each Other

Helpers who bear witness to many stories of abuse and violence notice that their own beliefs about the world are altered and possibly damaged by being repeatedly exposed to traumatic material.

**—Karen Saakvitne and Laurie Anne Pearlman**
*Transforming the Pain*, p. 49

In this chapter, you are invited to:

- Read the following article and discuss it with your supervision group and/or work colleagues
- See whether there are ways for you to use Low-Impact Debriefing in your personal and professional life

## After a Difficult Session ...

Are you debriefing *all over* your colleagues? Do your colleagues share graphic details of their days with you?

Can you still properly debrief if you don't give all the graphic details of the trauma story you have just heard from a client? Would you like to have a strategy to gently prevent your colleagues from telling you too much information about their trauma exposure?

When helpers hear and see difficult things in the course of their work, the most normal reaction in the world is to want to debrief with someone, to alleviate a little bit of the burden that they are carrying. It is healthy to turn to others for support and validation. One problem is that we are often not doing it properly. Another problem is that colleagues don't always ask us for permission before debriefing their stories with us.[1]

**RESPECTING PATIENT AND CLIENT CONFIDENTIALITY**

In some helping professions, patients and clients must sign a consent form indicating whether you have permission to discuss their clinical issues or any content of their file before you discuss their particular case with anyone else. Clients can also clearly specify with whom you are allowed to discuss their case. Respecting client confidentiality is paramount. Even if you have consent, make sure that you are not releasing identifying information unnecessarily. If you live in a small community, it can sometimes be very easy for your colleagues to identify the client you are speaking of. Ask yourself: "how much information do I need to share in order to debrief? Is it really necessary to mention the client's name in this instance, or his occupation?" Taking these extra steps will protect your clients' paramount right to privacy and confidentiality.

## Two Kinds of Debriefing

Many helpers acknowledge that they occasionally share sordid and sometimes graphic details of the difficult stories they have heard with one another in formal and less formal debriefing situations. Debriefing is an important part of the work that we do: it is a natural and important process in dealing with disturbing material.

There are two kinds of debriefing that occur among helpers: (1) the informal debriefing, which often takes place in a rather ad hoc manner, whether it be in a colleague's office at the end of a long day, in the staff lunchroom, in the police cruiser, or during the drive home; and (2) the debriefing that is a more formal process and is normally scheduled ahead of time and referred to as peer consultations, supervision, or critical incident stress debriefing.

Part of the problem with formal debriefing or scheduled peer supervision is the lack of immediacy. When a helper has heard something disturbing during a clinical day, they usually need to talk about it to someone then and there or at least during the same day. I used to work at an agency where peer supervision took place once a month. Given that I was working as a crisis counselor, I almost never made use of this time for debriefing (or much of anything else) because my work was very live and immediate. A month was a lifetime for the crises I witnessed. This is one of the main reasons why helpers take part in informal debriefing instead. They grab the closest trusted colleague and unload on them.

A second problem for some of us is the lack of satisfactory supervision. If I administered a satisfaction scale right after you left your supervisor's office, I am sure that you would be able to give me a rating on how useful that process was for you. Sadly, for many helpers, the score they would give their supervisor is often rather low for a variety of reasons (having insufficient time, skill level of the supervisor, the quality of your relationship with them, trust, etc.).

## Are You Being Slimed During Informal Debriefs?

The main problem with informal debriefs is that the listener, the recipient of the traumatic details, rarely has a choice in receiving this information. Therefore, they are being *slimed* rather than taking part in a debriefing process. Therein lies the problem and the solution.

## Contagion

Sharing graphic details of trauma stories can actually spread vicarious trauma to other helpers and perpetuate a climate of cynicism and hopelessness in the workplace. Helpers often admit that they don't always think of the secondary trauma they may be unwittingly causing the recipient of their stories. Some helpers (particularly trauma workers, police, and fire and ambulance workers) tell me this is a "normal" part of their work and that they are desensitized to it, but the data on vicarious trauma (VT) show otherwise.

## Four Key Strategies to Avoid Retraumatizing Our Colleagues and Loved Ones

In their book *Trauma and the Therapist: Countertransference and Vicarious Traumatization in Psychotherapy With Incest Survivors*, Laurie Anne Pearlman and Karen Saakvitne put forward the concept of "limited disclosure," which is a strategy to mitigate the contamination of helpers informally debriefing one another during the normal course of a day.[2]

I have had the opportunity to present this strategy to hundreds of helping professionals over the past decade, and the response has been overwhelmingly positive. Almost all helpers acknowledge that they have, in the past, knowingly and unknowingly traumatized their colleagues, friends, and families with stories that were probably unnecessarily graphic. Over time, we started referring to the strategy of limited disclosure as low-impact disclosure (LID) or low-impact debriefing. What exactly does LID look like?

Think of the traumatic stories you hear in your work as being contained behind a tap. I invite you to decide, via the process described below, how much information you will release and at what pace.

Let's walk through the process of the LID strategy. It involves four key steps: self-awareness, fair warning, consent, and low-impact debriefing.

### *Increased Self Awareness*

How do you debrief when you have heard or seen hard things?

Take a survey of a typical workweek and note all of the ways in which you formally and informally debrief with your colleagues. Note the amount of detail you provide them with (and the amount of detail they share with you), and the manner in which this is done: do you do it in a formal way, at a peer supervision meeting, or by the water cooler? What is most helpful to you in dealing with difficult stories?

## Fair Warning

Before you tell anyone a difficult story, you must give them fair warning. This is the key difference between formal debriefs and ad hoc ones: If I am your supervisor and I know that you are coming to tell me a traumatic story, I will be prepared to hear this information and it will be less traumatic for me to hear.[3] If I am casually chatting with a colleague about their weekend plans and you barge in and tell us graphic details of a sexual abuse story you just heard, we will be more negatively impacted by the details. In fact, we use fair warning in everyday life: If you had to call your sister and tell her that your uncle has passed away, you would likely start the phone call with "I have some bad news" or "You'd better sit down." This allows the listener to brace themselves to hear the story.

## Consent

After you have given warning to the listener, you need to ask for consent. This can be as simple as saying, "I need to debrief something with you; is this a good time?" or "I heard something really hard today, and I could really use a debrief; could I talk to you about it?" The listener then has a chance to decline or to qualify what they are able and ready to hear. For example, if you are my work colleague, I may say to you: "I have 15 minutes and I can hear some of your story, but would you be able to tell me what happened without any of the gory details?" or "Is this about children [or whatever your trigger is]? If it's about children, I'm probably the wrong person to talk to; but otherwise I'm fine to hear it."

## Limited Disclosure

Now that you have received consent from your colleague, you can decide how much of the tap to turn on. I suggest imagining that you are telling the story starting on the outer circle of the story (i.e., the least traumatic information) and slowly moving in toward the core (the very traumatic information) at a gradual pace. You may, in the end, need to tell the graphic details, or you may not, depending on how disturbing the story has been for you.

**QUESTIONS TO ASK YOURSELF BEFORE
YOU SHARE GRAPHIC DETAILS**

Is this conversation a:

Debriefing?
Case consultation?
Fireside chat?
Work lunch?
Parking lot catch-up?
Children's soccer game (Sadly, I have seen this.)
Christmas party?
Pillow talk?
Other …

Is the listener:

Aware that you are about to share graphic details?
Able to control the flow of what you are about to share with them?

If it is a case consultation or a debriefing:

Has the listener been informed that it is a debriefing, or are you sitting in
their office chatting about your day?
Have you given them fair warning?

## How Much Detail Is Enough? How Much Is Too Much?

Are you participating in a staff meeting or a case conference? Is sharing the graphic details necessary to the discussion? Sometimes it is, but often it is not. For example, when discussing a child being removed from the home, you may need to say, "the child suffered severe neglect and some physical abuse at the hands of his mother," and that may be enough, or you may in certain instances need to give more detail for the purpose of the clinical discussion. Don't assume you need to disclose all the details right away.

I would recommend applying this approach to all conversations you have. Ask yourself: Is this too much trauma information to share?

Low-impact debriefing is a simple and easy VT protection strategy. It aims to sensitize helpers to the impact that sharing graphic details can have on themselves and on their colleagues.

**SOME ADDITIONAL SUGGESTIONS**

■ Experiment with low-impact debriefing and see whether you can still feel properly debriefed without giving all the gory details. You may find that at times you do need to disclose all the information; this is often an important process in staying healthy as helpers. At other times, however, you may find that you did not need to disclose all the details.

■ Organize an educational session followed by a discussion at your workplace about the concept of low-impact debriefing.

**MAKING IT PERSONAL HOMEWORK**

Consider bringing this chapter on low-impact debriefing to work and discussing it with your colleagues. Failing that, discuss it with your peer support group. How might low-impact debriefing be received in your respective places of work? Could you identify two or three colleagues who might be willing to adopt LID?

If you wish to provide your colleagues with more information, you can download and print copies of an article that outlines the steps to LID by visiting my Web site: http://compassionfatigue.ca/category/resources/articles-to-download/

## What to Expect

Like any other boundary-setting, not everyone will welcome this strategy. All those of you who are social workers, psychologists, and mental health counselors, return to your Family Therapy 101 course. Remember what Minuchin and his friends said about family systems? That systems like status quo and that most systems are highly resistant to change, even if this change is for the better in the long term. The same applies to this new strategy. Expect some resistance among your co-workers, but don't give up.

## Endnotes

1. Mathieu, F. (2008). Adapted from a post on my blog http://compassionfatigue.ca/low-impact-debriefing-how-to-stop-sliming-each-other/
2. Pearlman, L.A., & Saakvitne, K.W. (1995). *Trauma and the therapist: Countertransference and vicarious traumatization in psychotherapy with incest survivors.* New York: W.W. Norton.
3. Rothschild, B. (2006). *Help for the helper: The psychophysiology of compassion fatigue and vicarious trauma.* New York: W.W. Norton.

## Chapter 6

# Warning Signs of Compassion Fatigue and Vicarious Trauma

When you're in the red zone of compassion fatigue, a bath ain't gonna cut it!

**—Robin Cameron**
*(Personal communication, 2003)*

In this chapter, you are invited to:

- Gain a clearer understanding of your own warning signs of compassion fatigue (CF) and vicarious trauma (VT)
- Develop an early detection system for your warning signs
- Identify your "red zone" of CF and VT

I was recently at the drugstore with my 10-year-old son.[1] I was paying for my purchase when an elderly man approached the counter. He appeared to be in his late 80s and had deep red bags under his eyes. He looked, in a word, absolutely terrible. With a shaking hand, he took a photo out of his pocket and showed it to us and to the women behind the cash register. "This is my wife," he said. "She died 2 days ago; we were married for 58 years. She was the love of my life. Now I can't sleep and the doctor wants me to take these pills." We all fell silent for a minute, and then I had a little chat with him. He told me his children all lived out of town and that he was completely alone. When I left the store with my son in tow, I felt regret that I did not do more. My head was already buzzing with all the community resources I know about, how to link him with the right ones, how we should have taken him out for tea, and more. I was dying to case manage this man into getting support right on the spot, but I also had to go home and cook dinner and take care of my family.

This is the constant challenge we face as helpers. Pain and suffering is all around us; it's not just at work. Where do you draw the line? Do you take every elderly widower out for tea? Do you tell every person with a funny-looking mole to go get it checked out? Do you rescue every kitten you see? So what we do is try our best to figure out boundaries. Sometimes we overcorrect and we become like Fort Knox, not letting a single person inside our walls. Sometimes we go too far in the other direction and become ambulance chasers, fostering too many pets and baking for every little old lady on our street.

We need to gain a better understanding of our own warning signs along the continuum of compassion fatigue. Using traffic lights as an analogy, the green zone is where you are when you are at your very best (I sometimes joke that you are only in the green zone when you've been in the field for 2 weeks or when you have just returned from a 5-month yoga retreat in Tahiti). The yellow zone is where most of us live most of the time. We have warning signs emerging but we often ignore them. The red zone is the danger zone. The far end of the red zone finds us on stress leave, clinically depressed or totally withdrawn from others and wracked with anxiety.

We will all visit the less extreme end of the red zone several times in our career—it is a normal consequence of doing a good job.

What suffers first is our emotional and physical health, our family and friends, our colleagues, and eventually our clients. They pay the price as we become less compassionate and irritable, and may make clinical errors.

Learning to recognize your own symptoms of compassion fatigue and vicarious trauma has a twofold purpose: First, it can serve as an important check-in process if you have been feeling unhappy and dissatisfied but did not have the words to explain what was happening to you; and second, it can allow you to develop a warning system for yourself. Developing this warning system allows you to track your levels of emotional and physical depletion. It also offers you tools and strategies that you can implement right away. Let me give you an example:

Say that you were to learn to identify your compassion fatigue symptoms on a scale of 1 to 10 (10 being the worst you have ever felt about your work/compassion, and 1 being the best you have ever felt). Then, you learn to identify what an 8 or a 9 looks like *for you*. For example, "When I'm getting up to an 8, I notice it because I don't return phone calls, I think about calling in sick a lot, and I can't watch any violence on TV," or "I know that I'm moving toward a 7 when I turn down my best friend's invitation to go out for dinner because I'm too drained to talk to someone else, and when I stop exercising." Being able to recognize that your level of compassion fatigue is creeping up to the red zone is the most effective way to implement strategies immediately before things get worse.

But look back to what also emerges in this process: you are starting to identify the solutions to your depletion.

If I know that I am getting close to an 8, I may not take on new clients with a trauma history, I may take a day off a week, or I may return to seek my own therapist.

Back to my story about the elderly man in the drugstore—I would not have always had this warm compassionate reaction to this man. In fact, my reaction is actually a sign for me that I am well out of the red zone of compassion fatigue (for the time being!). You see, there have been times where I have felt so depleted by all my work demands and difficult stories that I would have hardened myself to this old man's story and not talked to him at all. Have you ever noticed that in yourself, or thought, am I the only hard, crusty person out there? Conversely, for some of you, being in the red zone would mean you would have jumped into rescuing this man and neglected your family's needs for the evening.

Research shows that compassion fatigue hits hardest among those of us who are the most caring.[2] As helpers, we have a homing device for need and pain in others and we have this from childhood onward (for many reasons: family of origin issues, birth order, heredity, etc.) So often for helping professionals the main challenge in their personal life is setting limits and not being a helper or rescuer to everyone around. But eventually, compassion fatigue makes us detach from others: often our colleagues, family, and friends suffer far before our clients and patients. Although I am not proud of it, I know that I always seem to save the best for work and give the remaining crumbs to my loved ones. In my clinical work, I feel present, warm, and loving toward my clients, even with the most challenging soldier who has never wanted to come to counseling and hates being there. But when I am in the red zone, I avoid my neighbors, ducking into my house as quickly as possible to avoid a chat, feeling slightly guilty and irritated at the same time.

Each of us will have different warning signs. The key to developing an early intervention plan is to get better acquainted with your own warning signs.

## Your Symptoms

To develop your warning scale, you need to develop an understanding and an increased awareness of your own symptoms of compassion fatigue and vicarious trauma. CF and VT will manifest themselves differently in each of us. In *Transforming the Pain*, Saakvitne and Pearlman have suggested that we look at symptoms on three levels: physical, behavioral, and psychological. Here is a list of warning signs based on a review of the literature to date.[3] I suggest that you begin by reading through the signs and symptoms below and circle those that feel true to you. Remember, this is not a diagnostic test but rather a process whereby we begin to understand our own physical and psychological reactions to the work that we do.

### *Physical Signs of Compassion Fatigue*

- **Physical exhaustion.** Feeling exhausted when you start your day, dragging your feet, coming back to work after a weekend off, and still feeling physically drained. Lipsky calls it, "feeling fatigued in every cell of your being."[4] It's also important to make the distinction between feeling tired and feeling depleted. I know that one of the ways for me to know that I'm struggling with depletion is that I lose my sense of humor at home and I turn into a drill sergeant. When I'm simply tired, I may need to slow things down at home, but I am still a person I like. Sometimes we are exhausted both emotionally and physically by the work.

- **Insomnia or hypersomnia.** Difficulty falling asleep, early morning awakening, or oversleeping.
- **Headaches and migraines.**
- **Increased susceptibility to illness.** Getting sick more often.
- **Somatization and hypochondria.** *Somatization* refers to the process whereby we translate emotional stress into physical symptoms. Examples are tension headaches, low back pain, gastrointestinal symptoms, stress-induced nausea, unexplained fainting spells, and so forth. The ailments are very real, but the root cause is largely related to emotions and stress. Someone I know has an upset stomach every time she is anxious or stressed. She used to think it was food poisoning but finally had to come to the conclusion that not all restaurants in our fine city could possibly have tainted food.

Think about which part of your body tells you that you are overloaded. What do you normally do when you get that migraine, eye twitch, or heartburn? Most of us take a pill, ignore it, and keep going. However, eventually, the body keeps the score (to borrow an expression from Bessel van der Kolk). In his book *When the Body Says No: The Cost of Hidden Stress,* Gabor Maté writes about the connection between chronic stress, repressed emotions, and physical illness and states: "Our immune system does not exist in isolation from daily experience."[5] He cites numerous stunning examples of ways in which the immune system is depleted by chronic stress.

*Hypochondriasis* refers to a form of anxiety and hypervigilance about potential physical ailments that we may have (or about the health of our loved ones). When it is severe, hypochondria can become a debilitating anxiety disorder. Mild versions of hypochondria can happen to many of us who work in the health care field. If you work in cancer care, particularly at the diagnostic end, you may find yourself overworried about every bump and bruise on your child or yourself, or you may think that everyone with a headache has a brain tumor. The media and the Internet can fuel the flames of hypochondria. Many people who live in Ontario say that they had some mild phantom symptoms of listeria during the summer of 2008 following a large-scale recall of tainted meat due to contamination.

*Again, any of these symptoms do not, on their own, constitute a serious problem. The goal here is for you to begin to notice your own susceptibilities and how the work that you do may be contributing to these vulnerabilities.*

## Behavioral Signs and Symptoms

- **Increased use of alcohol and drugs.** There is evidence that many of us are relying on alcohol, marijuana, or over-the-counter sedatives to unwind after a hard day. Have you seen the size of wine glasses these days? Some of them are bigger than my fishbowl. So the "one glass after work" you are having is possibly half a bottle of wine. Even if you are not addicted to drugs or alcohol, if you are relying on a drink or other substance every night to unwind, then you are likely self-medicating your stress away.

  The difficulty with increased reliance on drugs and alcohol is also that there may be a lot of shame associated with it, and it is not something that we necessarily feel we can disclose to anyone. Is the child protection worker going to tell his supervisor that he smokes a big fat joint every night when he gets home to unwind? Is the nurse going to tell her colleagues that she takes a few Percocets here and there from her mother's medicine cabinet?

- **Other addictions** (shopping, workaholism, compulsive overeating).

- **Absenteeism** (missing work).

- **Anger and irritability.** Anger and irritability are considered two of the key symptoms of compassion fatigue. This can come out as expressed or felt anger toward colleagues, family members, clients, chronic crisis clients, and others. You may find yourself irritated with minor events at work: hearing laughter in the lunch room, announcements at staff meetings, the phone ringing. You may feel annoyed and even angry when hearing a client talk about how they did not complete the homework you had assigned to them. You may yell at your own children for not taking out the garbage. The list goes on and on, and it does not add up to a series of behaviors that make you feel good about yourself as a helper, a parent, or a spouse.

  Try this: Spend a full day tracking your anger and irritability. What do you observe? Any themes or recurrences? Any situations you regret in hindsight or where your irritability was perhaps out of proportion?

- **Exaggerated sense of responsibility.** "I can't leave; people are counting on me."[6] In her book *Trauma Stewardship*, Laura van Dernoot Lipsky suggests that helpers can develop "an inflated sense of importance related to one's work" and become addicted to the need to be needed: "Many people get hooked on involvement in others' lives: solving their problems, becoming a powerful figure for them, getting increasingly attached to the feeling of being needed and useful."[7]

- **Avoidance of clients.** Examples of this can be not returning a client's phone call in a timely fashion, hiding in a broom closet when you see a challenging family walking down the hall, delaying booking a client who is in crisis even though you should see them right away. Again, these are not behaviors that most of us feel proud of or that we are comfortable sharing with our colleagues and supervisors, but they do sometimes occur and then we feel guilty or ashamed, which feeds into the cycle of compassion fatigue.

Many of us work with some very challenging clients. If you do direct client work, I am sure that you can easily conjure up, right now, the portrait of an individual or a family that has severely taxed your patience and your compassion. One telephone crisis worker I once spoke to put it perfectly: "Why on earth is it a thousand times easier for me to talk to 25 different crisis callers in a day than if the same caller calls me 25 times in a row? I am, after all, paid to answer the phone and talk to individuals in crisis for 7 hours a day. That's my job. What is so depleting about the chronic caller?" And, I would add, why do we start feeling particularly irritated, avoidant, and unempathetic toward the chronic caller? The fact of the matter is that there is something inherently depleting about chronic crises. The best solution, if we cannot control our caseload, is to seek more training. The more we understand chronicity, the more compassion we can retain.

■ **Impaired ability to make decisions.** This is another symptom that can make a helper go underground. Helpers can start feeling professionally incompetent and start doubting their clinical skills and ability to help others. A more severe form of this can be finding yourself in the middle of an intervention of some kind, and feeling totally lost, unable to decide what should happen next. I once had a mild version of this indecisiveness in the middle of a grocery store for what felt like hours after a grueling clinical day (I was working as a crisis counselor at the time and was dealing with very extreme situations and a very large volume of demand). I remember standing in the middle of the grocery store thinking, should I buy the chocolate chip cookies or the lemon creams? and being unable to decide between the two for what felt like hours. Difficulty making simple decisions can also be a symptom of depression.

■ **Forgetfulness.** Many of us lead busy, hectic lives. Forgetting to turn off the coffeemaker once in a while is normal for all of us, but leaving the house without the baby can be a sign of overload.

■ **Problems in personal relationships.** Avoiding social events with friends; not returning phone calls from your loved ones because you are too tired or emotionally exhausted; hearing complaints from your family, who find that you are frequently irritable and emotionally unavailable. Over time, you can become more socially isolated and lose important connections with others.

■ **Attrition.** Helpers leaving the field, either by quitting or by going on extended sick leave.

■ **Compromised care for clients.** This can take many forms: using the label *borderline* for some clients as a code word for *manipulative* is one common example. Whenever a diagnosis is being used in a way that pigeonholes a client, we are showing our inability to offer them the same level of care as other clients. There is evidence that clients with a BPD label (borderline personality disorder) frequently do not receive adequate care in hospitals, are not assessed for suicidal ideation properly, and are often ignored and patronized. Granted, clients with personality disorders can be extremely difficult to work with, but when we lose compassion for them and start eye-rolling when we see their name on our roster, something has gone awry.

If you ever have the opportunity to go hear Dr. John Briere present, I highly recommend that you do. Dr Briere is a leader in the field of trauma treatment and research, with a particular specialization in working with individuals who have experienced childhood trauma. He is the director of the psychological trauma program at Los Angeles County and University of South California medical center. During his talks, Dr. Briere presents a wonderful perspective on the use (or rather, the misuse) of the diagnosis of BPD. He believes that the term is used to label clients who are in chronic emotional distress as difficult and draining (which they can be) but that the field is also misusing it as a dismissive and damaging label. He argues that a very large proportion of clients diagnosed with BPD have in fact complex post-traumatic stress disorder (PTSD), not BPD, and are very damaged because of their trauma experiences. They end up being revictimized by a system that cannot cope with their complex and frequent needs.[8]

There are many other examples of compromised care for clients but I think this is a particularly illustrative one:

## "WE DON'T GET ENOUGH TRAINING:" A STORY OF COMPLEX PTSD

"Anne" is a 51-year-old woman who had a number of medical problems for which she was regularly in and out of the hospital. She had been seen by a number of physicians over the previous years. She was a woman with severe lung disease, COPD (chronic obstructive pulmonary disease). She had been in and out of emergency and ICU at times for her lung issues. She also had diabetes, chronic pain, high blood pressure, depression, and anxiety.

Anne was on high doses of painkillers for her joint and muscle pain. Her diagnosis was arthritis but her pain was often muscular as well. When I first met her, I explained that I found that she was on a lot of medications and that when I see someone who has a lot of pain issues that are not well controlled in spite of adequate doses of pain medications, I always ask about a history of abuse or trauma.

In this first clinic visit with me, Anne broke down and disclosed that she had been sexually assaulted by her uncle and then her brother from age 7 to age 14. Her mother did not believe her when she told her. Anne finally ran away at the age of 14. Anne stated that she had never told anyone other than her current husband about this. She stated that the multiple medical providers that she had come in contact with had never asked her about a history of trauma.

As I got to know Anne, she displayed the classic behaviors of complex PTSD with the anxiety, affect dysregulation, depression, somatization. I was very surprised and disappointed that the medical system that she was involved in regularly had failed to identify this major underlying issue. This case very much exemplifies that complete lack of understanding of the issue of complex PTSD. Medical professionals are not trained to understand complex PTSD. Many have probably never even heard of it and yet these "problem" patients are often interacting with the traditional medical system where their somatic issues are poorly dealt with, only to recur again and again.

**—As told by a family physician**

■ **The silencing response.** Eric Gentry and Anna Baranowsky—pioneers in the field of compassion fatigue research—put forward a concept called the *silencing response*. The silencing response is a process whereby we unknowingly silence our clients because the information they are sharing with us is too distressing for us to bear. The more we suffer from compassion fatigue, the more likely we are to use the silencing response: "The Silencing Response ... is an inability to attend to the stories/experiences of our clients and instead to redirect to material that is less distressing for the professional. This occurs when client's experiences/stories are overwhelming, beyond our scope of comprehension and desire to know, or simply spiraling past our sense of competency. The point at which we may notice our ability to listen becoming compromised is the point at which the Silencing Response has weakened our clinical efficacy."[9]

Some examples of the silencing response are: "changing the subject, avoiding the topic, providing pat answers, minimizing client distress, boredom, feeling angry with the client, using humor to change or minimize the subject, faking interest or listening, not believing clients and not being able to pay attention to your clients."[10] An excellent full-length article by Anna Baranowsky about the silencing response appears in Charles Figley's book *Treating Compassion Fatigue*.

## Psychological Signs and Symptoms

■ **Emotional exhaustion.** A hallmark of compassion fatigue.
■ **Distancing.** You find yourself avoiding friends and family, not spending time with colleagues at lunch or during breaks, and become increasingly

isolated. You find that you don't have the patience or the energy or interest to spend time with others.

■ **Negative self-image.** Feeling unskilled as a helper; wondering whether you are any good at this job; feeling negative about yourself as a spouse, a parent, or a friend.

■ **Depression.** Depressed mood, difficulty sleeping or oversleeping, impaired appetite, loss of interest in activities, fatigue and loss of energy, feelings of hopelessness and guilt, suicidal thoughts, difficulty imagining that there is a future.

■ **Reduced ability to feel sympathy and empathy.** This is a very common symptom among experienced helpers. Some describe feeling numb or highly desensitized to what they perceive to be minor issues in their clients or their loved ones' lives. The old stereotype is the doctor who lets his child walk around with a broken arm for 3 days before taking him to hospital because he has missed the symptoms and minimized them as a slight sprain, or oncology nurses who deal with patients in severe pain who feel angry or irritated when a family member complains of a non-life-threatening injury.

Reduced ability to feel empathy can also occur if you are working with a very homogeneous client population. After seeing hundreds of 20-year-old university students come through my crisis counseling office, I noticed two things happening: One, I would silently jump ahead of their story and fill in the blanks ("I know where this story is going"). Two, if I had just seen someone whose entire family had died in an automobile accident, I found it very difficult to summon up strong empathy for a student whose boyfriend had just broken up with her after 2 weeks of dating.

There are of course inherent risks associated with this reduced empathy and jumping ahead. Clients are not all the same, and we risk missing a crucial issue when we are three steps ahead of them. We always need to navigate the fine line between not being ambulance chasers who think every single person is a suicide risk and being numb to the point that we fail to ask basic risk assessment questions to everyone, including the person who looks just fine. The good news is that the solution to this is very simple: vary your caseload to stay fresh and stay on top of your professional development.

■ **Cynicism and embitterment.** Eye-rolling at the brand-new nurse who is enthusiastically talking about an upcoming change or idea she has to improve staff morale, groaning when seeing a certain client's name on your roster, and cynicism toward your children's ideas or enthusiasm.

Unfortunately, cynicism is rampant in high-stress environments such as health care and prisons. You may find yourself feeling cynical toward your colleagues, your clients, and your family and friends. Or you may be working in a very negative work environment where you are surrounded by cynical colleagues. Laura van Dernoot Lipsky writes: "cynicism is a sophisticated coping mechanism for dealing with anger and other intense feelings we may not know how to manage."[11]

■ **Resentment.** Resentment of demands that are being put on you by others, of fun events that are being organized in your personal life; feeling irritated with your best friend for calling you on your birthday; resentment of having to take an extra shift because your colleague is away on stress leave. Resentment can eat away at us like a poison and turn us into angry, brittle people. This in turn has a direct impact on the workplace atmosphere (and the mood in your home).

■ **Dread of working with certain clients.** Do you ever look at your roster for the day and see a name that makes your stomach lurch, where you feel total anticipatory dread? Is this happening with greater frequency?

■ **Feeling professional helplessness.** Feeling increasingly that you are unable to make a difference in your clients' lives. Being unable to help because of situational barriers, lack of resources in the community, or your own limitations. Some client situations are very complex and the chaos in their lives can run deep. Sometimes it is very hard for us as helpers to hang on to a thread of hope.

■ **Diminished sense of enjoyment/career** (i.e., low compassion satisfaction).

■ **Depersonalization.** Dissociating during sessions with clients. Again, this is a matter of frequency—many of us space out once in a while, and this is normal; but if you find that you are dissociating on a more frequent basis, it could be a symptom of VT. Have you ever driven home and not remembered the drive from work to your house? Most of us have done this more than once. Now how about this: have you even driven home from work, not remembered the drive home, and found that your car was filled with groceries you had no recollection purchasing?

■ **Disruption of world view/heightened anxiety or irrational fears.** This is one of the key symptoms caused by vicarious traumatization. When you hear a traumatic story, or 500 traumatic stories, each one of these stories has an impact on you and your view of the world. Over time, your ability to see the world as a safe place is severely impacted. You may begin seeing the world as an unsafe place. Some examples of this are: A counselor who works with children who have been sexually abused becomes unable to hire a male babysitter for fear that the sitter will abuse her children. A physician forbids his children to ever chew gum after seeing a tragic event happen with a child and gum at his work. A prison guard develops a fear of home invasion after working with a serial rapist. An acquired brain injury therapist develops a phobia of driving on the highway after too many motor vehicle accident rehabs.

A recent workshop participant told me that after working at a youth homeless shelter, she became obsessed with monitoring her teenage children's every move, convinced that they were using drugs and having unprotected sex. She finally realized she had gone too far when she started lecturing her 10-year-old son's friends about methamphetamines and condoms, only to see their horrified faces at the breakfast table.

Some of this is inevitable. We call VT and CF occupational hazards for this very reason: As Laurie Anne Pearlman says, it is not possible to open our hearts and minds to our clients without being deeply affected by the stories they tell us. But what is important to notice is how severe these disruptions have become for you. We can also sometimes mitigate the impact by doing restorative activities (e.g., working with healthy children, working on a quilt for people with AIDS).

■ **Increased sense of personal vulnerability.** See above.

■ **Inability to tolerate strong feelings.** Read about the silencing response above. This can also occur with family, friends, and colleagues.

■ **Problems with intimacy.** As a couples counselor I heard many stories about relationship challenges including differences of opinion about money management, parenting, household chores, in-laws, and sex and intimacy. Many helpers confess that they come home completely uninterested in the idea of having sex with their spouses. As one client said to me, "I come home, after giving and giving to all of my patients all day. Then I give to the kids, then I clean up and get ready for the next day. Finally, it's 9:30 p.m. and all I want to do is collapse in bed with a trashy novel. Then my husband comes upstairs and wants to have sex, and I feel like saying, 'Are you kidding me? I'm all done. Please leave me alone.'" And these are not necessarily couples with significant preexisting marital problems. The depletion caused by the job *is* the problem. Of course, better communication and educating spouses about the realities of CF can help greatly. Helpers who work with sexual abuse survivors may also find that their work intrudes on their ability to enjoy a healthy sexual relationship with their partner.

■ **Hypervigilance.** When I run workshops, I can always tell which participants work in law enforcement: they always sit with their backs to the wall and a clear view of the door. Why do they do this? If you ask them, they will tell you that it's second nature to them, they simply have a reflex to sit somewhere where you can see any incoming (i.e., potentially threatening) person and also be able to get out of the room rapidly if there ever was an emergency. This is a form of hypervigilance that has been learned on the job. Some prison staff also tell me that they are more fearful of home invasions and have developed a ritual to secure their homes as a direct result of the work they do with inmates who specialize in breaking and entering. Many counselors who work in the field of sexual abuse describe feeling suspicious toward any male sports coach, cub leader, and so forth who approaches their child.

Trauma survivors often experience hypervigilance due to past trauma events (e.g., you had to hide whenever a siren sounded and now any sound that resembles a siren makes you go into a state of panic, or for a moment, without even thinking about it, you move to duck under a desk). As helping professionals, we can internalize our clients' high levels of alert. As Lipsky says, we can "feel like we're always 'on.' Even during times where there is absolutely nothing that can or should be done."[12]

■ **Intrusive imagery.** This is another symptom of vicarious trauma: Finding that your clients' stories are intruding on your own thoughts and daily activities. Some examples are having a dream that does not belong to you; having difficulty getting rid of a disturbing image a client shared with you; being unable to see a rope as a benign rope, after someone has shared a graphic suicide story with you; or having certain foods be unappealing to you after hearing about certain smells or sounds from a war veteran. It is not unusual for those intrusive images to last a few days after hearing a particularly graphic story, but when they stay with you beyond for more than a couple of weeks, you are likely having a secondary traumatic stress experience. (You can read an excellent description of this in Eric Gentry's article *Compassion Fatigue: A Crucible of Transformation*; see the Bibliography for more details).

■ **Hypersensitivity to emotionally charged stimuli.** Crying when you see the fluffy kittens from the toilet paper commercial; crying beyond measure in a session that is emotionally distressing (welling up is normal; sobbing is not).

■ **Insensitivity to emotional material.** Sitting in a session with a client who is telling you a very disturbing or distressing story of abuse, and you find yourself faking empathy, while inside you are thinking either, I've heard much worse, or, Yup, I know where she is going with this story; I wonder what's for lunch at the canteen.

I know a wonderful family doctor who eventually realized that she was struggling with VT. She used to share, at our dinner table, extremely graphic stories of medical procedures of horrible growths or cancerous tumors (usually in the nether regions) with our 3- and 5-year-old children sitting with us. She seemed completely unaware of the children's horrified looks on their faces, never mind the adults.

Other examples are finding that you are watching graphically violent television and it does not bother you in the slightest, while people next to you are recoiling in horror.

■ **Loss of hope.** Over time, there is a real risk of losing hope—losing hope for our clients (that they will ever get better) and maybe even hope for humanity as a whole.

■ **Difficulty separating personal and professional lives.** I have met many helping professionals who, quite frankly, have no life outside of work. They work through lunch, rarely take their vacations, carry a beeper or smart phone at all times, and are on several committees and boards related to their work. They are also always on call to help their family and are the "caregiver extraordinaire" for everyone around them. I once knew a helping professional who carried her work cell phone at all times. I used to see her at daycare, frequently answering client calls at 7:30 a.m. while dropping her children off. I was very curious about this and asked her later what her working hours were and she said proudly, "Oh, I start at 9 a.m. but clients can reach me any time of day or night." This person worked at the local hospital and belonged to a large roster of social workers there, with their on-call beepers on a rotating basis. None of the other social workers at the hospital took client calls at 7:30 a.m. unless they were at work or on call, but she had lost the ability to separate her professional life from her personal life.

■ **Failure to nurture and develop non-work-related aspects of life.** Many of the helpers that I meet confess that they have lost touch with the hobbies, sports, and activities they used to enjoy. Some tell me that they collapse in bed at the end of their workday, too tired to consider joining an amateur theater group, go curling, or join a book club. Yet "having a life" has been identified as one of the key protective elements to remaining healthy in this field.

### EXERCISE: DEVELOPING AN EARLY WARNING SYSTEM

I believe that compassion fatigue is a normal consequence of working in the helping field. The best strategy to address compassion fatigue is to develop excellent self-care strategies, as well as an early warning system that lets you know that you are moving into the caution zone of CF.

Self-care is not something we figure out once and for all and get the certificate and put it on our wall. You can't say, "I completed a course and now I'm a certified expert in my own self-care."

You know how radiology technicians wear a little widget (called a dosimeter) that monitors how much radiation they have been exposed to? That's what I visualize we should all wear: a little self-care wellness dosimeter, (Figure 6.1).

It would always be on, and it would beep once when we're getting slightly overloaded, twice when we are headed for a big doozy of a week, and maybe give us an electric shock when we're headed for a total crash!

I would now like to you try to visualize your own self-care wellness dosimeter: What would it look like for you? What would be a symbolic way for you to regularly take stock and check in with yourself?

**Figure 6.1   Self-care wellness dosimeter.**

Most of us have a built-in warning system for general stress: for example, I get tight in the shoulders and neck when I'm starting to get overloaded; my best friend gets a migraine. You can probably name your own symptoms, but do you know what your CF warning signs are?

With the image of your dosimeter in mind, try to visualize that you place it back in its dock every night. This dock downloads the stress and trauma exposure you have had and gives you a reading.

In reality, this can be a 2-minute "how am I doing today?" process, or maybe for you it's journaling at the end of the day, or a simple "how did my day rate on a scale of 1–5?"

This is why learning to recognize one's own symptoms of compassion fatigue can serve as an important check-in process, as it can allow us to develop a warning system for ourselves. Being able to recognize that one's level of compassion fatigue is creeping up to the red zone allows us to implement strategies rapidly before things get worse.

### *MAKING IT PERSONAL* HOMEWORK

After reading through the list of warning signs, spend 15 minutes completing this writing exercise. If you are working with a group, consider sharing some of your signs and symptoms with one another.

### MY WARNING SIGNS: WRITING EXERCISE

1. What signs and symptoms stand out most for me?
2. What signs and symptoms do I bring home with me most often?
3. What signs and symptoms do I experience at work?
4. What do I have to lose if I don't deal with the effects of this occupational hazard?
5. What do I stand to gain if I move toward improved self-care?
6. Who will be the biggest supporters of my self-care?

**RECOMMENDED READING**

To read more on signs and symptoms:

Figley, C.R. (Ed.). (1995). *Compassion fatigue: Coping with secondary traumatic stress disorder in those who treat the traumatized.* New York: Routledge.

Pearlman, L.A., & Saakvitne, K.W. (1995). *Trauma and the therapist: Countertransference and vicarious traumatization in psychotherapy with incest survivors.* New York: W.W. Norton.

van Dernoot Lipsky, L. & Burk, C. (2009). *Trauma stewardship: An everyday guide to caring for self while caring for others.* San Francisco: Berrett-Koehler.

In her book *Trauma Stewardship*, Laura van Dernoot Lipsky has an excellent conceptualization of symptoms, which she calls, "The 16 warning signs of trauma exposure response." (p. 47)

## Endnotes

1. Mathieu, F. (2010). Adapted from a blog post published on www.compassionfatigue.ca. http://compassionfatigue.ca/moving-out-of-the-red-zone-of-compassion-fatigue-getting-feeling-back-in-our-toes/
2. Figley, C.R. (Ed.). (1995). *Compassion fatigue: Coping with secondary traumatic stress disorder in those who treat the traumatized.* New York: Routledge.
3. Saakvitne, K.W., Pearlman, L.A., & the staff of the Traumatic Stress Institute. (1996). *Transforming the pain: A workbook on vicarious traumatization.* New York: W.W. Norton; Pearlman, L.A., & Saakvitne, K.W. (1995). *Trauma and the therapist: Countertransference and vicarious traumatization in psychotherapy with incest survivors.* New York: W.W. Norton; Figley, C.R. (Ed.). (1995). *Compassion fatigue: Coping with secondary traumatic stress disorder in those who treat the traumatized.* New York: Routledge; Gentry, J.E., Baranowsky, A.B., & Dunning, K. (1997). Accelerated recovery program for Compassion Fatigue. Paper presented at the meeting of the International Society for Traumatic Stress Studies, Montreal, Quebec, Canada; van Dernoot Lipsky, L. & Burk, C. (2009). *Trauma stewardship: An everyday guide to caring for self while caring for others.* San Francisco: Berrett-Koehler.
4. van Dernoot Lipsky, L. & Burk, C. (2009). *Trauma stewardship: An everyday guide to caring for self while caring for others.* San Francisco: Berrett-Koehler, p. 81.
5. Maté, G. (2003). *When the body says no.* Toronto: Vintage Canada, p.6.
6. van Dernoot Lipsky, L. (2009). p. 111.
7. van Dernoot Lipsky, L. (2009). p. 111.
8. For more information on complex PTSD, see: Courtois, C.A., & Ford, J.D. (2009), *Treating complex traumatic stress disorders.* New York: Guilford Press.
9. Gentry, J.E., Baranowsky, A., & Dunning, K. (1997). http://www.tir.org/research_pub/research/compassion_fatigue.html
10. Baranowsky, A.B. (2002). The silencing response in clinical practice. In C.R. Figley (Ed.), *Treating compassion fatigue.* New York: Brunner-Routledge.
11. van Dernoot Lipsky, L. (2009). pp. 103–104.
12. van Dernoot Lipsky, L. (2009). p. 65.

## Chapter 7

# Contributing Factors: Understanding How Your Job Is Impacting You

> To combat compassion fatigue and burnout, agency administrators and therapists may also wish to ask themselves, "How many cases are too many?"[1]
>
> **—Kyle D. Killian**

In this chapter, you are invited to:

- Gain a better understanding of the factors that contribute to your compassion fatigue (CF) and vicarious traumatization (VT)
- Complete a self-assessment checklist to identify your primary contributing factors

## Why Do We Get CF/VT? Contributing Factors[2]

As we discussed in earlier chapters, compassion fatigue exists on a continuum, meaning that at various times in our careers, we may be more immune to its damaging effects and at other times feel very depleted by it. Within an agency, there will be, at any one time, helpers who are feeling healthy and fulfilled in their work, a majority of people who are feeling some symptoms, and a few people feeling like there is no other answer available to them but to leave the profession. The main factors contributing to this continuum are your personal and current life factors and your work situation.[3]

## *Personal and Current Life Factors*

Your current life circumstances, your childhood history, your way of coping with stress, and your personality all affect how compassion fatigue and vicarious trauma will impact you.[4] In addition to working in a challenging profession, most helpers have other life stressors to deal with. Many of us belong to the "sandwich generation," meaning that we take care of both young children and aging parents. Helpers are not immune to pain in their own lives, and in fact some studies show that we are more vulnerable to life changes such as divorce and difficulties such as addictions than people who do less emotionally stressful work.

## *Relationship to or Close Identification With Those Being Assisted[5]*

For helpers who work in small communities, it can be hard to draw a clear line between work and home life. In the past few years, I have had the privilege of working with the Department of Justice Victim Service Division in the Yukon and Northwest Territories, where there are staggering rates of abuse and trauma. Some of the victim service workers are tasked with assisting victims in preparing a victim impact statement and accompanying them to court. This, in and of itself, can be challenging for helpers in terms of trauma exposure. But in remote communities, the offender *and* the victims *and* the support worker can often all be related to one another. This can place the worker in real ethical dilemmas, and they often get pitted against part of the community when advocating for a victim. In addition, resources are very scarce in small northern villages. The victim service worker can end up having to work extra-long hours, offering support that is often outside the scope of their training.

## *Working Conditions*

Recent studies clearly show that the volume of work (a high caseload) and lack of control over the workload are directly related to lower compassion satisfaction.[6] Moreover, quality supervision is not always available to all helpers.

Clients and their stories are not always the main source of stress—it's also the paperwork, the new computerized system staff have to learn, and, let's not forget, the nth restructuring/merging with the agency next door/new executive director/best practice remodel that an agency is going through for the fourth time in 8 years. Helpers participating in my workshops often say, "I don't have any problems with my clients/patients; in fact, I love my clinical work. It's everything around it that is grinding me down." Moreover, helpers often do work that other people don't want to hear about, or spend their time caring for people who are not valued or understood in our society such as individuals who are homeless, abused, incarcerated, or chronically ill. The working environment is often stressful and fraught with workplace negativity as a result of individual compassion fatigue and unhappiness. We will discuss this further in the next chapter.

For mental health counselors, the push for the exclusive use of evidence-based practice (EBP) is presenting some additional challenges. EBP is the use of "manualized, empirically tested interventions that demonstrate evidence of ameliorating psychological symptoms."[7] The use of EBP comes from the medical field, where it makes sense to adopt a strict treatment protocol (I certainly would want that if I needed surgery—there is clearly research that demonstrates the best way to operate on my heart, for example, and I would hope the cardiology clinic I visit adheres to this.) This may sound like a great idea for psychology and counseling as well, but applying EBPs to mental health treatment is far more complicated than it sounds: Data show that in psychological counseling, there is no one-size-fits-all approach that works for every client. Research also shows that the best approaches are those that use the therapeutic techniques in the larger context of the relationship with the client. As Scott Miller recently said: "Is this relationship between this consumer and this provider, program, level of care, working for this individual at this time and place?"[8] No rigid, manualized treatment approach can guarantee that in mental health counseling. The moral distress caused by having to blindly adhere to EBPs can only make matters worse for the helping professional (and, I would suggest, for the client).

## INTERESTED IN READING MORE ON EVIDENCE-BASED PRACTICE?

Scott Miller is a clinical psychologist who specializes in assessing service delivery in behavioral health. His passion is in client-directed, outcome-informed clinical work. He is a prolific writer and a gifted workshop presenter. He recently founded the International Center for Clinical Excellence (centerforclinicalexcellence.com).

I also recommend that you read:

Farley, A.J., et al. (2009). The challenges of implementing evidence based practice: Ethical considerations in practice, education, policy and research. *Social Work & Society,* (7) 2.

## A HOSPITAL SOCIAL WORKER REFLECTS

*Over my 23-year career I have learned the importance of self-care and work/life balance and pride myself on my ability to look after myself in the midst of doing very difficult trauma work. However, I was recently reminded of how quickly the tides can turn in the constant ebb and flow of compassion fatigue. In the midst of massive organizational change, I quickly learned how the balance can be toppled. I was shocked and embarrassed by my level of paranoia as my program was being bulldozed in the face of making improved overall changes. For weeks I sat in my office literally shaking, waiting for management to come with the cardboard box and escort me out of the building. I started to clean out my office myself and bring important things home because I was so convinced that the knock on the door was coming. The stress of this was so overwhelming that I finally came to a place where I was fantasizing for it to occur already so that I could experience some relief and get on with my life. I have always found that I could function well doing the difficult work of trauma counseling as long as my team and organization were stable. When this stability was no longer there, I found I could not function in supporting my clients because I was feeling that I was the one in need of support. Ultimately the support of family, peers, and friends was the connection I needed to sustain me and be the voice of reason amidst all my exaggerated fears.*

**—Hospital social worker**

## Risk of Personal Injury

As discussed in Chapter 4, a large number of helping professionals are assaulted or threatened in the line of duty.

## Insufficient Training

Work overload means that helpers are often asked to do work that is outside of their scope of practice. We are sometimes asked to run a program after having had barely enough training ourselves to feel confident with the material.[9]

## Working in Isolation

More helpers are being asked to work with ever-decreasing resources in smaller and less well organized teams. Kyle Killian found that social support at work was "the most significant factor associated with compassion satisfaction."[10] This

### HOW DID YOU LEARN ABOUT SELF-CARE?

In his study of trauma counselors and compassion fatigue, Kyle Killian found that "most of the therapists interviewed observed that they had not had any courses or specific training on professional self-care, and this was an important but neglected area in training."[11] He recommends that self-awareness and self-care become integral parts of the curriculum for all helping professionals.

finding is both encouraging and concerning as we know that compassion fatigue erodes what we most need: our connection with others. Burnout, compassion fatigue, and vicarious trauma can contribute to poor workplace morale and bitterness. The more embittered we are, the less likely we are to turn to our colleagues for support (or for *constructive* support—we may spend a lot of time bitching to them about the work, but is this productive and healthy?). Killian strongly recommends that we create structured group meetings to offer one another regular support.

## *Let's Stop Blaming the Helpers*

Killian and others before him found that individual self-care strategies were only moderately effective in reducing CF and VT in helpers. Killian is concerned that by focusing only on individual self-care, we risk falling into the pitfall of blaming the helpers for developing CF and VT: "This focus implies that helping professionals who are hurting are somehow at fault—they are not balancing work and life."[12] Far more effective were organizational changes that offered helpers better working conditions, more control over their schedule, good-quality supervision, and reduced exposure to trauma.

Killian believes that our industry as a whole has to make a "paradigm shift" where we see the solution to CF and VT in a larger (organizational, political, societal) context rather than focusing solely on individual helpers' responsibility to self-care: "As trainers, educators, and supervisors, we want to protect therapists from compassion fatigue, enhance their resilience, and help professionals deliver quality mental health interventions, but to achieve these goals, we may need to shift paradigms, moving our focus away from individualistic efforts at education and training and toward a more systemic approach of advocacy for healthier working conditions."[13]

---

### *MAKING IT PERSONAL* HOMEWORK: ASSESS YOUR CONTRIBUTING FACTORS

In their book *Transforming the Pain*, Saakvitne and Pearlman offer a conceptual way to assess contributing factors. They divide them up in the following manner:

Nature of the Work
Nature of the Clientele
Nature of the Helper

Within Nature of the Work, the authors ask helpers to assess elements such as:

- Do you have control over your schedule?
- Are you satisfied with your current schedule?
- Do you have a healthy workplace?
- Do you like your work?
- Do you feel supported in your workplace?
- Do you have support from colleagues at work, or within your profession?
- Are you getting enough helpful supervision?

Within Nature of the Clientele, the authors ask helpers to assess elements such as:

- Does your work with clients feel fulfilling?
- Do you get to see clients improve?
- Do you feel well suited for this work?
- Do you feel well trained to do your job?
- Is there balance and variety in your workday?
- Do you have clients you enjoy working with?

Within Nature of the Helper, the authors ask helpers to assess elements such as:

- Do you have a fulfilling social life?
- Are you able to make time for yourself?
- Do you have non-work-related hobbies/activities?
- Do you have healthy coping strategies?
- Are you aware of your own family history/past traumas and how this may impact your work and your own well-being?

*Question:* What are your thoughts about your current job and how it contributes to your compassion fatigue? Take your journal or a separate sheet of paper to answer these questions. If you are working with a group, consider sharing some of findings with one another.

Adapted from Saakvitne, K.W., Pearlman, L.A., & the staff of the Traumatic Stress Institute. (1996). *Transforming the pain: A workbook on vicarious traumatization.* New York: W.W. Norton. pp. 53–55.

**RECOMMENDED READING**

Killian, K.D. (2008). Helping till it hurts? A multimethod study of compassion fatigue, burnout, and self-care in clinicians working with trauma survivors. *Traumatology*, (14) 2.

www.headington-institute.com. The Headington Institute is an organization that offers Web-based and in-person training and support to humanitarian relief and aid workers across the world. They provide excellent free resources for all helping professionals, regardless of whether you are an aid worker or not. I highly recommend you visit their Web site.

Saakvitne, K.W., Pearlman, L.A., & the staff of the Traumatic Stress Institute. (1996). *Transforming the pain: A workbook on vicarious traumatization*. New York: W.W. Norton, pp. 32–44.

## Endnotes

1. Killian, K.D. (2008). Helping till it hurts? A multimethod study of compassion fatigue, burnout, and self-care in clinicians working with trauma survivors. *Traumatology*, *14*(2), 41.
2. This section is adapted from an article entitled, "Running on Empty," originally published in the Spring 2007 issue of *Rehab & Community Care Medicine*.
3. Saakvitne, K.W., Pearlman, L.A., & the staff of the Traumatic Stress Institute. (1996). *Transforming the pain: A workbook on vicarious traumatization*. New York: W.W. Norton, pp. 53–59.
4. Saakvitne, K.W., Pearlman, L.A., & staff. (1996).
5. The Headington Institute, "Understanding and Addressing Vicarious Trauma Self-Study Course." http://www.headington-institute.org/Default.aspx?tabid=2649
6. Killian, K.D. (2008). Helping till it hurts? A multimethod study of compassion fatigue, burnout, and self-care in clinicians working with trauma survivors. *Traumatology*, *14*(2), 32–44.
7. Craig, C.D., & Sprang, G. (2010). Compassion satisfaction, compassion fatigue, and burnout in a national sample of trauma treatment therapists. *Anxiety, Stress & Coping, 23*(3), 322.
8. Miller, S.D. (2011). Transforming public behavioral health care: Improving outcome and efficiency with consumer-driven, outcome-informed service delivery. Presented at the Canadian Counseling and Psychotherapy Association's annual conference, Ottawa, May 2011.
9. Pearlman, L.A., & Saakvitne, K.W. (1995). *Trauma and the therapist: Countertransference and vicarious traumatization in psychotherapy with incest survivors*. New York: W.W. Norton.
10. Killian, K.D. (2008). p. 40.
11. Killian, K.D. (2008). p. 42.
12. Killian, K.D. (2008). p. 42.
13. Killian, K.D. (2008). p. 43.

## Chapter 8

# The Toxic Workplace

Every larger system has an obligation to the people who make it work, as well as to the people it serves. At the same time, each of us must recognize that we have a role to play in shaping the organizations and social systems we participate in.

**—Laura van Dernoot Lipsky**
*Trauma Stewardship* (p. 17)

In this chapter, you are invited to:

- Identify strategies to improve your work environment
- Work through an activity called *Taming the Dragon* with your colleagues to help you identify your yellow zone at work

## Dealing With Negativity at Work

Many helping professionals have told me that one of their biggest challenges at work is their colleagues' cynicism and negativity. Workplace toxicity is a common consequence of compassion fatigue (CF), vicarious traumatization (VT), and burnout in our field. As discussed earlier, research shows that a helper is far less likely to develop severe VT and CF if they work in a highly supportive work environment with reasonable caseloads, regular access to peer support, and control over their schedule.[1] Of course, there are difficult and stressful jobs in any field—airline customer service representatives are said to have one of the most stressful jobs in the service industry, for example. But the helping fields have the added burden of being exposed to traumatic stories, individuals in distress, and a huge volume of work as a matter of course.

When a workplace is toxic, several things happen: The atmosphere becomes one of mistrust (with the suspicion often directed at upper management). Many of us get locked into a negative frame of mind and we start turning on each other (this is also known as the "must be nice" phenomenon, which we will discuss later). Unfortunately, we often take it out on our newest recruits. Several years ago, at the end of a presentation in a psychiatric hospital, a rather intimidating senior nurse approached me at the podium and said, "You know, I had never realized until today's workshop that I am burned to a crisp. I am like a little strip of bacon with two white shoes and a white hat! I have been a psychiatric nurse for over 30 years and you know what I do? I try and toughen up the young nurses as quickly as possible, because I don't want them to suffer like I did. I tell them to suck it up, showing your emotions is not professional. But now I realize that I am probably burning them out." There is a terrible expression in nursing that you may have heard before: "nurses eat their young," and so far, of the thousands of nurses I have met during my trips across the country, not one of them has disagreed. This form of horizontal violence is symptomatic of the helplessness we get locked into—we turn on each other rather than trying to collaborate to advocate for change.

## Have You Gotten Stuck in a Negative Rut?

Lipsky says that some of us start clinging to our feelings of bitterness and a sense of having been wronged and persecuted—and as a result we lose the belief in our ability to make a change:[2]

> We become convinced that others are responsible for our well-being and that we lack the personal agency to transform our circumstances. This notion has less to do with our physical surroundings than with our internal state. We may believe that we deserve better pay, safer work environments, more respect, adequate time away from work, and greater resources, and all this may be true … [but] we can succumb to a belief that we have no capacity to influence any outcome.[3]

When I worked in a busy student counseling center several years ago, two of my colleagues and I noticed that we had fallen into a bad pattern: after staff meetings, we used to go straight into a nearby office and have a debrief about the meeting. But in truth, this was mostly a bitch session about our colleagues, management, and the university as a whole. After a while, we started noticing that these debriefs were not helpful to us. We weren't contributing to making a positive change; we were just complaining to each other. So we deliberately decided to stop gossiping about work for 3 months, and the result was striking: We were not necessarily successful at changing our dysfunctional workplace, but we were no longer part of the toxicity, and that significantly improved my work experience.

## THE BMWS

A dear colleague of mine refers to these bitch sessions as the *BMWs* (bitching, moaning, and whining). The problem with the BMWs is that it is a bit like a fake workout. Have you ever had a fake workout? A fake workout is when you sit down on the couch, watch a yoga DVD, and eat a bag of chips. The results? Not what you are hoping for.

## WHEN BURNOUT TAKES A LIFE OF ITS OWN: EMBITTERMENT[4]

A few years ago Michael Linden coined a new term he called *posttraumatic embitterment disorder*,[5] which, he says, occurs in some people following a single negative life event that continues to cause prolonged bitterness, anger, feelings of injustice, and distress for an extended period of time. (He gives Captain Nemo from Jules Verne's book *20,000 Leagues Under the Sea* as an example, if you can cast your mind back to your childhood readings.) Linden's patients had great difficulty letting go of feeling wronged and would spend an inordinate amount of time ruminating about the circumstances surrounding the emotional injury. It became a debilitating obsession for them.

I am not a big fan of pathologizing human emotions, so I am not particularly interested in the "disorder" aspect of Linden's observations (nor has it been accepted by the field as an actual diagnostic category), but I do think he makes a very good point about the risk for some of us of getting locked into a pattern of obsessing about wrongs done to us. I have encountered this quite frequently among clients who were incredibly bitter about an ugly divorce and simply could not let it go, even several years later. I also saw this in individuals who felt wronged by their workplace. When I worked for the military, I always knew which clients were experiencing workplace embitterment. They would invariably walk into our first appointment with reams of papers documenting their fight for justice in light of a perceived wrong: a promotion denied, receiving a black mark on their performance appraisal, being reprimanded for something they had not done. They were often right—an abuse of justice *had* taken place—but what was striking was their obsessiveness—they were consumed by this event and could not move on, even if it cost them their health, their marriage, and their career.

So, without necessarily adopting Linden's diagnostic label, I invite you to reflect on this—are you holding on to something that may be causing you more harm than good? Seeking the help of a personal counselor can be very helpful in helping you grieve the loss and pain you are feeling.

## Dealing With Your Colleagues' Dragons

Many of us have to work with challenging (even at times toxic) colleagues. Given this reality, I invite you to reframe this negativity and think of it as an organizational form of compassion fatigue, caused by the CF and VT that some of our most depleted colleagues are experiencing. My friend Robin Cameron refers to it as our dragon: "I like to think of it as a dragon that all helping professionals carry on their shoulder. Sometimes the dragon is very small and green (we have little or no CF/VT), sometimes it is big and red and pulsating (we are really burned out) and we breathe fire all over our colleagues, and sometimes it is medium-sized and yellow (that's most of the time for most of us)."

This dragon impacts our colleagues and our loved ones, even when we think we are hiding our CF successfully and "faking it" through a workday.

The first step in learning to deal with your colleagues' dragons is to gain a better understanding of your own dragon and its various states—how do you behave toward your colleagues when you are in the red zone of compassion fatigue?

---

### *MAKING IT PERSONAL* HOMEWORK: "TAMING THE DRAGON" EXERCISE

This activity can be done solo, with your peer group, or with your work colleagues.

Think about what your dragon looks like when you are in the yellow/red zone.

What is he like? What is he thinking (what would be the thought bubble)? Is he breathing fire at other co-workers or clients or kids/friends? Is he dark or bright? How much space does he take in the office?

If you are working as a group, take turns with the following:

■ Tell the group something about your dragon. What does your dragon look like when he is in the yellow zone? In the red zone?

■ Tell us what your CF/VT looks like in terms of behaviors with co-workers and what is helpful in those situations. How can we help (by giving you some space, or by being more present, etc.)?

■ What would you be like if you came to work one day and your dragon wasn't there? How would you be different?

Then hold a brainstorming conversation:

■ How do we cope at the office? Can we look at creating strategic alliances?

■ How can we develop concrete strategies as a team? Regular meetings/communication board?

■ Could we implement physical exercise during lunch breaks/other?

■ How do we know when we need a professional team from outside of the agency to help us through a traumatic situation?

■ Share ideas for ensuring continuity of progress: plan monthly check-ins/other?

---

### ONE AGENCY'S CF-REDUCTION INITIATIVE

What do you think about what this agency is trying to do or has done already? What might work for you?

*"We have made self-care and team care a team agenda for each meeting. In response to this, the two small offices meet in the morning for breakfast, and one of the offices goes to lunch as a group on Wednesdays. Office A tries to have lunch each day and to go for walks, and Office B is in the process of defining how they will do this. They have agreed to bring in a yoga instructor in January for 8 weeks, to work out on their lunch hour—this will cost them each $5 per session. Our Staff Development Team is in the process of purchasing some guided relaxation DVDs and CDs for staff to use on their lunch hours as well, and we recently purchased a number of yoga mats for Office B."*

## Endnotes

1. van Dernoot Lipsky reports findings from a study by Golie Jansen at Easter Washington University that found that "when people perceive their organizations to be supportive, they experience lower levels of vicarious trauma." Jansen, Golie (2004) Vicarious trauma and its impact on advocates, therapists, and friends. *Research & Advocacy Digest, 6*(2), p. 21.
2. van Dernoot Lipsky, L., & Burk, C. (2009). *Trauma stewardship: An everyday guide to caring for self while caring for others.* San Francisco: Berrett-Koehler.
3. van Dernoot Lipsky, L. (2009). p. 93.
4. Thank you to Dr. Peter Huggard for this.
5. Linden, M. (2003). Posttraumatic embitterment disorder. *Psychother. Psychosom., 72*(4): 195–202.

# Chapter 9

## Addressing CF and VT: Strategies

The question is *not* whether stress will appear and take a toll on those working as clinicians. Instead, it is to what extent professionals take the essential steps to appreciate, limit and learn from this very stress to continue—and even deepen their personal lives and roles as helpers and healers.

**—Robert J. Wicks**
*The Resilient Clinician*, p. 14

In this chapter, you are invited to:

■ Identify strategies to mitigate your own compassion fatigue (CF) and vicarious traumatization (VT) on three levels: professional, organizational, and personal

## Preventing Compassion Fatigue: Is it Possible?

There is much debate among CF researchers about the notion of *prevention*. Personally, I don't think that there is really such a thing as CF and VT prevention—I do not believe that you can work in this field for any length of time without being profoundly impacted by the stories you hear and gradually depleted by the work (unless you see only one client per week and spend the rest of your time doing yoga and meditation!).

However, I do think that CF and VT can be mitigated, transformed, and treated and that there are ways to replenish ourselves so that we can have a long and rewarding career. These are solvable problems providing we recognize the signs and symptoms early and that the intervention is appropriate to the level of CF and/or VT present in the helper.

## What Has Been Found to Help Reduce Compassion Fatigue?

Research in the field shows that the following key strategies have been found to reduce compassion fatigue and vicarious trauma in helping professionals:

- Strong social support both at home and at work
- Increased self-awareness
- Good self-care
- Better work/life balance
- Job satisfaction
- Rebalancing caseload and workload reduction
- Limiting trauma inputs (see Chapter 11)
- Accessing coaching, counseling, and good clinical supervision as needed
- Attending regular professional development and ongoing training

Saakvitne and Pearlman[1] suggest that strategies and solutions can be implemented on three levels: *professional, organizational,* and *personal.* In addition, I believe that changes need to occur on a broader societal level with more funding to healthcare and social services, a greater recognition of the work that we do, and improved salaries and working conditions for helping professionals. Figure 9.1 provides a visual guide of Saakvitne and Pearlman's model for implementing strategies both at home and at work.

## Professional and Organizational Strategies[2]

There are many simple and effective organizational and professional strategies that helpers can implement to protect themselves from compassion fatigue. First, by openly discussing and *acknowledging* that compassion fatigue occurs in the workplace, helpers can normalize this problem for one another. They can also work toward developing a supportive work environment that will encourage proper *debriefing,* regular breaks, mental health days, *peer support,* assessing and changing workloads, improved access to further professional development, and regular check-in times where staff can safely discuss the impact of the work on their personal and professional lives.

Research has shown that *working part-time,* or only seeing clients or patients part-time and doing other activities during the rest of the workday, can be a very

**Figure 9.1   The three levels of strategies and solutions.**

effective method to mitigate the impact of compassion fatigue. This can mean actually working part-time or working two different jobs: for example, working as a counselor 3 days a week and in a bookstore 2 days per week or splitting your job 50/50 between direct patient care and some other work at the same agency. You could, for example, job share a front-line position with someone and spend the other half of your time doing education and training or program development. This not only reduces your exposure to difficult client stories, it also gives you an opportunity to replenish yourself.

> *I have been blessed with the ability to make changes in my life. Six months ago I left my full-time position and dropped to part-time. It was the biggest decision I have had to make in my life, but I feel transformed. I had been living in the red zone for a long time. I know that I made the right decision for myself and my family and also for those I care for in my place of employment. I feel like a better nurse as well as a better mother. I have a beautiful 3-year-old boy at home. I look around at my colleagues and I see so much suffering and depleted, lifeless personalities. I want to help them. I want to be the positive person who can make a change. I am not sure how to apply this to my work environment, but I will definitely attempt to do so. Change terrifies so many, but the little changes can make a big difference.*

**—Megan Price, registered practical nurse, long-term care facility**

Continuing education and *adequate training* have also been shown to be extremely protective for helpers. Adequate training refers to specific skill acquisition that helpers need to master to do their work effectively and with confidence. As discussed earlier, many of us are often asked to do work that is outside the

---

### RECOMMENDED READING

#### GOING DOWN TO 80% CAN MAKE A BIG DIFFERENCE TO YOUR WELL-BEING.

Research shows that working 4 days per week instead of 5 does not lead to a major difference, if any, in take-home pay. Having that extra day off might allow you to run errands, rest, exercise, and catch up on life.

I invite you to read more on this topic:

A brief description of this strategy can be found in Patrick Fanning's book *50 Best Ways to Simplify Your Life.*

For a more thorough exploration of this and related concepts, I recommend reading *Your Money or Your Life: Transforming Your Relationship With Money and Achieving Financial Independence,* third edition, revised for the 21st century, by Joe Dominguez and Vicki Robin (2008).

**A SIDEBAR ABOUT TRAUMA WORK**

When I present to a large audience of helping professionals, I often ask for a show of hands of who in the room is a trauma counselor or a trauma worker. Unless I am at a trauma conference, very few people raise their hands. I then ask for a show of hands of who in the room has received trauma training. Again very few hands normally go up. Finally, I ask for everyone in the room who works with clients who have experienced trauma to raise their hands and usually a large majority of the participants raise their hands! If we work with trauma survivors, we need more tools to deal with the trauma.

scope of the formal training we have received in our trade. We "learn by doing" and can at times feel that we are flying by the seat of our pants. Helpers with severe compassion fatigue often speak of feeling de-skilled and incompetent. Another obstacle has to do with diminished resources, particularly in small communities. In rural areas, a helping professional may end up wearing many hats that push the limits of their areas of competence. In addition, *ongoing professional development* and skill building is imperative throughout our careers as helpers. Researchers in the field of CF and VT have identified that attending regular professional training is one of the best ways for helpers to stay renewed and healthy. There are of course several benefits to this: connecting with peers, taking time off work, and building on your clinical skills.

Identify an area of expertise that you want to hone. If you are not able to travel to workshops, consider taking online courses. CPR and first aid are techniques that require recertification on a regular basis. Why should we not do the same with other clinical techniques that we use in our work?

More work needs to be done to parse out details: What are the key resiliency factors? How many hours a week of direct client care is optimal? What debriefing methods have proven to be the most effective? Hopefully, researchers will soon bring us some more answers.

## Personal Strategies

Improved self-care is the cornerstone of mitigating the impact of compassion fatigue. This may seem obvious, but many helpers tend to put their needs last and feel guilty for taking extra time out of their busy schedules to exercise, meditate, or have a massage. On the personal front, you need to carefully and honestly assess your life situation: Is there a balance between nourishing and depleting activities in your life? Do you have access to regular exercise, nonwork interests, personal debriefing? Are you a caregiver to everyone, or have you shut down and cannot give any more when you go home? Are you relying on alcohol, food, gambling, shopping to de-stress? We must recognize that ours is highly specialized work and our home lives must reflect this.

As discussed in Chapter 6, *having access to good social support*, both at home and at work is highly protective.

*A helper's own history of abuse* will make them more vulnerable to VT. Accessing regular counseling and supervision can help counterbalance this vulnerability.

## Self-Awareness

> When we keep ourselves numbed out on adrenaline or overworking or cynicism, we don't have an accurate internal gauge of ourselves and our needs.
>
> **—Laura van Dernoot Lipsky[3]**

Earlier in this book, I referred to Dr. Gabor Maté's work *When the Body Says No.* I highly recommend reading this powerful book on the connection between chronic stress and illness. One of the key messages in Dr. Maté's work is on the importance of self-awareness—not just being aware of our current feelings, actions, and reactions but also being aware of the dynamics from our past that influence the everyday choices we make. Dr. Maté also emphasizes the importance of gaining an understanding and awareness of how we deal with anger, hurt, and resentment. In my clinical training, I often heard the saying that depression is "anger turned inward." Given the incontrovertible evidence we now have of the connection between our physical health and our emotional states, imagine what happens to our immune system when we push our emotions away? (Please read his book for a far more eloquent explanation of this phenomenon.)

### *What Does Self-Awareness Actually Mean?*

Self-awareness means being in tune with your stress signals. Do you have a good sense of how your body communicates to you when it is overwhelmed? Do you get sick as soon as you go on vacation, develop hives, get a migraine when you are stressed? Many of us live in state of permanent overload and are dimly aware of it. What happens when you feel angry? Do you explode or do you swallow your rage? Where in your body do you feel your anger?

Self-awareness also means being aware of how your past influences your current life and work choices—why did you choose to go into this field and not another? Did you pick this profession because of a trauma or loss you experienced in your own life? Were you already a helper in your family of origin? Are you the go-to person in your personal life? Do you feel empty or unimportant unless you are in a helping role? Self-awareness also means understanding how your own childhood history affects your reactions to your clients' stories (this is also known as *countertransference*).

Are you aware of the ways in which you sabotage your self-care (by saying yes to requests you don't have time for, by taking on more responsibilities, by drinking excessively, by canceling a therapy appointment, etc.)?

## Two Important Principles for Staying Afloat

Eric Gentry, compassion fatigue scholar and co-developer of the Accelerated Recovery Program (ARP) for helpers with compassion fatigue, wrote a powerful article in 2002 called "Compassion Fatigue: The Crucible of Transformation."[4] I highly recommend that you read it.

In this article, Gentry offers two important principles that are critical to remaining healthy in the face of the challenges of our work:

> These two important principles, which have become the underlying goals for our work in the area of compassion fatigue, are: (1) the development and maintenance of intentionality, through a non-anxious presence, in both personal and professional spheres of life, and (2) the development and maintenance of self-validation, especially self-validated caregiving. We have found, in our own practices and with the caregivers that we have treated, that when these principles are followed not only do negative symptoms diminish, but also quality of life is significantly enhanced and refreshed as new perspectives and horizons begin to open.[5]

Let us highlight the two key concepts from that paragraph: "(1) the development and maintenance of intentionality, through a non-anxious presence, in both personal and professional spheres of life, and (2) the development and maintenance of self-validation, especially self-validated caregiving." What does this mean exactly?

*A non-anxious presence* refers to the ability to be in the room with the client's pain and suffering and be able to express empathy and compassion without taking on the client's suffering. In both the personal and the professional realm, it is about mindfulness, the ability to notice and control your physical symptoms of stress and anxiety, and your breathing. It is a concept that is explored in depth by Babette Rothschild, author of *Help for the Helper: The Psychophysiology of Compassion Fatigue and Vicarious Trauma*. We will talk about Rothschild's work in a later section.

*Self-validated caregiving* refers to self-care that is guilt-free, self-care that is prioritized as a means of remaining healthy in this line of work. These two concepts form the foundation of compassion fatigue protection, which we will discuss in more detail in the following chapters.

## TRANSITIONING FROM WORK TO HOME[6]

Do you have a transition ritual when you leave work?

Do you have a transition time between work and home? Do you have a 20-minute walk through a beautiful park, or are you stuck in traffic for 2 hours? Do you walk in the door to kids fighting, or do you walk into a peaceful home?

Some helpers change clothes when they get home, go for a run, sing in the car, meditate, and so forth. Others acknowledge that they don't do anything: they may even come home and go straight back to their laptops to continue working.

Helpers have told us that one of their best strategies involved a transition ritual of some kind: putting on cozy clothes when getting home and mindfully putting their work clothes "away" as in putting the day away as well, having a 10-minute quiet period to shift gears, or going for a run. One workshop participant said that she had been really missing going bird watching, but that her current life with young children did not allow for this. She then told us that her new strategy would be the following: From now on, when she got home from work, instead of going into the house right away, she would stay outside for an extra 10 minutes, watching the activity in her birdfeeders.

Do you have a transition ritual? If not, can you think of something you could start implementing in your daily routine?

## *MAKING IT PERSONAL* HOMEWORK

### DEVELOPING A COMPASSION FATIGUE PROTECTION TOOLKIT FOR YOURSELF

In my workshops, I encourage helpers to design a toolkit that will reflect their own reality and that will integrate their life circumstances and work challenges. This is a very individual process—your self-care strategies may not work for your neighbor and vice versa. Here are some key questions to ask yourself to begin the process:

What would go in my CF protection toolkit?
What are my warning signs—on a scale of 1 to 10, what is a 4 for me? What is a 9?
Scheduling a regular check-in, every week. When will it take place?
What things do I have control over?
What things do I not have control over?
What *stress relief* strategies do I enjoy? Examples of stress relief are taking a bath, sleeping well, or going for a massage.

What *stress reduction* strategies work for me? Stress reduction means cutting back on things in our life that are stressful (switching to part-time work, changing jobs, reworking your caseload, etc.).

What *stress resiliency* strategies can I use? Resiliency strategies are relaxation methods that we develop and practice regularly, such as meditation, yoga, or breathing exercises.[7]

---

**RECOMMENDED READING**

To read more on the concepts discussed in this chapter, I recommend:

Gabor Maté. (2003). *When the Body Says No: The Cost of Hidden Stress*. Toronto: Random House.

Gentry, E. (2002). Compassion fatigue: A crucible of transformation. *Journal of Trauma Practice, 1*(3/4), 37–61.

Morgenstern, J. (2004). *Never check email in the morning and other unexpected strategies for making your work life work*. New York: Fireside.

Lillie Weiss. (2004). *The Therapist's Guide to Self-Care*. New York: Brunner-Routledge.

Timothy Ferriss. (2009). *The 4-Hour Workweek*. New York: Random House.

---

# Endnotes

1. Saakvitne, K.W., Pearlman, L.A., & the staff of the Traumatic Stress Institute (1996). *Transforming the pain: A workbook on vicarious traumatization*. New York: W.W. Norton.

2. This section is adapted from an article entitled "Running on Empty," originally published in the Spring 2007 issue of *Rehab & Community Care Medicine*. Mathieu, Françoise. (2007). Running on empty: Compassion fatigue in health professionals. *Rehab & Community Care Medicine*, Spring 2007.

3. van Dernoot Lipsky, L. & Burk, C. (2009). *Trauma stewardship: An everyday guide to caring for self while caring for others*. San Francisco: Berrett-Koehler. p. 131.

4. Gentry, E.J. (2002). Compassion fatigue: The crucible of transformation. *Journal of Trauma Practice, 1*(3/4), 37–61.

5. Gentry, Eric. (2002).

6. Saakvitne, K.W., Pearlman, L.A., & staff. (1996).

7. Thank you to Robin Cameron for the concepts of stress relief, reduction, and resiliency.

# Chapter 10

## The Four Steps to Wellness

In this chapter you are invited to:

- Read the Green Cross "Standards of Self-Care Guidelines," located in Appendix B, and discuss with your colleagues
- Learn the four steps to wellness to protect yourself from compassion fatigue (CF) and vicarious traumatization (VT)

There are four steps that you can take to reduce and transform your compassion fatigue and vicarious trauma:

1. Take stock of your stressors.
2. Look for ways to enhance your self-care and work/life balance.
3. Develop resiliency skills.
4. Make a commitment to implement changes.

The fourth step, make a commitment to implement changes, should occur throughout this process: as you take stock, learn new strategies for improved self-care, and acquire new resiliency skills, you are hopefully also making concrete commitments to make these changes real and lasting. In addition to this, you will be invited to make some commitments at the end of this workbook to help you take this further.

## Standards of Self-Care

Dr. Charles Figley is a trauma specialist based in the United States. He is known as the founding father of compassion fatigue research and has been closely involved in the development of trauma training and disaster relief. Along with his colleagues, he created the Green Cross Academy of Traumatology, initially as a

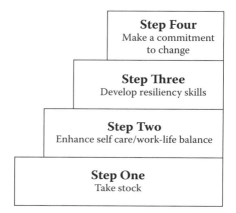

**Figure 10.1**

response to the Oklahoma City bombing of the Federal Building in 1995. Green Cross is a nonprofit organization that aims to offer humanitarian aid to disaster survivors as well as trauma and compassion fatigue education to first responders.

Green Cross created "Standards of Self-Care Guidelines," which provides a wonderful template for all of us helping professionals, regardless of whether we are first responders or not. Green Cross argues that self-care is an ethical imperative. They believe that it is in fact unethical for us *not* to attend to our self-care needs since we now know that insufficient self-care translates into poor-quality care for our patients and clients.[1]

The complete "Standards of Self-Care Guidelines" are included in Appendix B. I invite you now to take a moment to read them.

### *MAKING IT PERSONAL* HOMEWORK

**1. Take a minute to read the following few lines with care:**

The Green Cross "Standards of Self-Care Guidelines" stipulates[2]:
"First, do no harm to yourself in the line of duty when helping/ treating others. Second, attend to your physical, social, emotional, and spiritual needs as a way of ensuring high quality services for those who look to you for support as a human being."

What does this mean for you?
Green Cross invites us to make this commitment in a concrete way: "Make a formal, tangible commitment: Written, public, specific, and measurable promise of letting go of work in off hours and embracing rejuvenation activities that are fun, stimulating, inspiriting, and generate joy of life."

What would it look like, in your life, if you attended to your physical, social, emotional, and spiritual needs? Where would you start?

2. **Discuss the "Standards of Self-Care Guidelines" with your buddy/support group or with your co-workers**. How does your workplace rate in terms of supporting these ethical imperatives? How do you score, on a personal level, in adhering to these guidelines?

## Endnotes

1. Green Cross "Standards of Self-Care Guidelines." Reprinted with permission, www.greencross.org

2. Excerpted from Green Cross "Standards of Self-Care Guidelines."

# Chapter 11

## Step One: Take Stock— Track Your Stressors at Home and at Work

I started to look at the things on my plate and realized it was overflowing, so I made some changes. I spoke with the priest at the church where I am an honorary assistant and explained that I needed a break from celebrating, preaching, and leading Bible study and retreats. I also decided I needed to exercise and focus on keeping myself well, so I bought a treadmill to walk three times a week. I established a transition from work to home. However, the most beneficial thing I did was to begin to share my story with someone I trusted.

**—From a hospital chaplain**

In this chapter you are invited to:

- Explore the best ways to track your stress levels in your daily life, both at home and at work
- Take some of these activities back to your workplace and discuss with colleagues

Compassion fatigue specialists are unequivocal: the key strategies to tackle compassion fatigue (CF) and vicarious traumatization (VT) are deceptively simple. What they require first and foremost is a willingness to take an honest look at ourselves.

Anyone who has attended my workshops will know that "taking stock" is one of my favorite recommendations. Most of us spend far too much time racing around in our busy lives without stopping to take an internal inventory of how we are actually feeling.

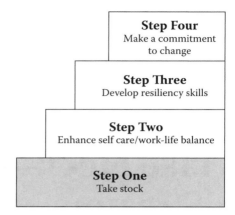

**Figure 11.1**

I have a client who is chronically overwhelmed—a true type-A workaholic. She once told me that she refuses to make to-do lists because they end up making her feel hopeless and discouraged. I have heard the same from clients who are deeply in debt. They will simply stop answering the phone as a way to deal with the creditors calling. We cannot do this with self-care and hope to stay in the field for the long haul. Something has got to give. Taking stock is therefore important.

## Tracking Your Physical Well-Being

*For me compassion fatigue is very much a physical experience due to my overactive fight/flight system that has symptoms of racing heart rate, breath, and thoughts. Because of this I really need to focus on physical outlets that release the adrenaline in my revved-up system but also lead by thoughts to refocus so I can relax. For me this means regular walks in the woods and, above all, ongoing yoga practice. As I have to concentrate on twisting my body into various pretzel shapes, it does not leave room for my thoughts to be intruded upon by my clients. In fact, my favorite part of yoga has now become* shavasana *or corpse pose at the end of my routine because it is only through yoga that I can create a truly quiet mind sometimes for 3 whole minutes. I have also found it useful to visualize my yoga routines when I cannot sleep, which helps me keep out the intrusive thoughts that are interrupting my sleep, and because I am focusing on a calming experience, it triggers my body to relax and turn off the fight/flight survival system.*

**—Diana Tikasz, social worker**

---

**WHERE TO FIND THE FULL BODY-SCAN EXERCISE**

**Web:** Through Google, I was able to find several audio and scripted body scan exercises in a matter of seconds. Here is a free body scan exercise script and audio: http://www.takingcharge.csh.umn.edu/activities/body-scan

**CD:** *Creating Inner Calm* by Mark Berber (only available at Indigo/Chapters, not Amazon)

**Books:** Bourne, E.J. (2000). *The Anxiety and Phobia Workbook, Oakland: New Harbinger.*

---

Do you have a good sense of how you are feeling physically today? Is there a part of your body that you have been neglecting or that has been causing you pain or discomfort lately? Have you recently had a medical checkup, dental exam, eyes checked?

The *body scan* is a very effective exercise from the field of relaxation training and stress reduction. The full version of the body scan encourages you to focus on each part of your body one after the other, to identify where you are holding tension. This process is normally done lying down, in a quiet room. There are examples of the full body scan in the shaded box above.

If time does not allow you to do the full scan, you can also carry out a modified version of the body scan:

> Sitting in a quiet, peaceful room, close your eyes and focus on your breathing. Notice what is happening in your body: Working your way down from the top of your head, notice how your jaw, neck, and shoulders are feeling at this moment. Remember to keep breathing, and if your mind wanders, gently bring it back. If that is all the time you have, take three slow, deep breaths through your nose and gently open your eyes. If you have more time, work your way down your body, noticing how your shoulders, arms, stomach, calves, and toes feel right now.

## Tracking and Limiting Your Trauma Inputs

Do you work with clients who have experienced trauma? Do you read about and see photos of and are generally exposed to difficult stories and images at your work? Take a survey of the trauma inputs of a typical day in your life. Starting at home, what does your day begin with? Watching morning news on TV? Listening to the radio or reading the paper? Note how many disturbing images, difficult stories, or actual photos of dead or maimed people you come across.

Now look at your work. Not counting direct client work, how many difficult stories do you hear, whether it be in a case conference, around the water cooler debriefing a colleague, or reading files?

Now turn your attention to your return trip home. Do you listen to the news on the radio? Do you watch TV at night? What do you watch? If you have a spouse who is also in the helping field, do you talk shop and debrief each other?

It is important to recognize the amount of trauma information that we unconsciously absorb during the course of a day. Many helpers say that they are unable to watch much of anything on television anymore, other than perhaps the cooking channel. Others say the reverse: they are so desensitized that they will watch very violent movies and shows and feel numb when others around them are clearly disturbed by it.

In our day-to-day life, we are exposed to a lot of extra trauma input outside of client work. We do not necessarily need to hear about all of these disturbing stories in graphic detail. We can create a "trauma filter" to protect ourselves from this extraneous material. (The idea of a "trauma filter" is discussed in Chapter 14 on developing compassion fatigue resilience.)

A great way to track your stressors is with the exercise called "what's on your plate," below.

---

### EXERCISE: WHAT'S ON YOUR PLATE?

Some of the questions were inspired by Cheryl Richardson's book *Take Time for Your Life*.[1]

Take a blank sheet of 8½ by 11 paper and draw a large dinner plate on it.

1. In your plate, write all the things you do/are responsible for, roles, jobs, responsibilities, life needs and issues presently. Write as many concrete details as possible. Think of a typical day in your life from start to finish (e.g., get up, make lunches for kids, make breakfast, clean up, call plumber, drive to work).
2. Look at the things within the plate you *would like to change and underline them* (don't worry whether or not they are actually changeable in reality at the moment).
3. Look at the things that are changeable at the moment *even by just 1%* and *circle these*. Think about what a 1% change could look like: If my goal is to improve my eating and lose 40 pounds, adding one apple per day to my diet could be a 1% change. If I want to start exercising, running a marathon would be a 100% change, walking around the block twice a week would be a 1% change.
4. On the outside of the plate, write down things you *wish you had more time for*.
5. When you had more time, perhaps when you were in high school or college, were there leisure activities you used to enjoy but have lost touch with (running, swimming, reading, singing, crafts)?

6. Think about why/how you did these things in the past.

7. Reflect on why you are not doing them now (or a 1% version of them—if you used to be a competitive figure skater, you may now enjoy skating once a week for fun?).

Ask yourself how can you make choices to integrate the things you wish you had more time for in your life now.

## GO FURTHER[2]

Choose one thing on your plate that you can delegate, say no to, back out of, or make one small step toward. For example, you have agreed to have your partner's family for a large family dinner and you identify this as the one thing on your plate you wish you could have said no to. Take 10 minutes to yourself and brainstorm every option you can think of, no matter how silly or unrealistic. Force your inner critic to sit out; when he or she starts to say, "No, you can't do that," tell her or him to be quiet while you finish the exercise. Your brainstorm list could be to call everyone back and tell them that you have a huge bug problem and the exterminator will be there; call and ask everyone to bring a dish rather than making dinner yourself; call and ask if this could be moved to another week after being honest about how tired you are feeling; ask your partner to make dinner for the family while you go out on the town with friends you haven't seen in a long time.

As you re-read your answers, and hopefully some of them are more outrageous than you would normally be, check your responses. For example, how did it feel to read the last one? Most of the helpers we work with have said that they would *never* back out of something they offered to do unless it was a life-or-death problem. Well, what does that say to your body? It says to your body, "Create a life-or-death problem for me so I can get out of things I don't want to do." Now you are really in a fix because your compassion fatigue may also be preventing you from standing up for yourself.

## REDUCING YOUR STRESS—TRYING TO SAY NO (OR YES)

If you have gone through your schedule and there really isn't even one area that could be lightened by even 1%, then it is time to, at the very least, stop taking on more.

*Say no to everything that is requested of you for 1 week.* I am not suggesting that you say no altogether, but always ask for time to think about it first. For bigger commitments, always ask for a night to sleep on it. For example, when someone asks me if I'm interested in taking on a new project, writing a new workshop, or presenting in a new city, I always take the time to think it over. In every circumstance I have been able to say something like, "That sounds really interesting; let me take a look at my calendar," or, "Let me talk to my partner and get back to you tomorrow or next week." If someone asks you to do something you are really game to do and you want to say yes—before you say yes, check in with your body and note how you feel. Through listening to your body you will be able to trust it to help you prioritize.

Go back to the "what's on your plate" exercise and quickly choose three things you wish you could change—any three items. Now, look critically at these three items and, for each one, ask yourself these three questions:

1. Is this something I have even a tiny bit of control over? (Some of the helpers we work with have chronic illnesses like diabetes. While they may not feel that they can control having diabetes, many have identified ways that they can honor their bodies and care for them more respectfully. For example: I will increase the number of fruits and vegetables that I eat every day.)
2. What would change in my life if this issue were to go away?
3. What 10% change could I make in this area?

Did one item stand out for you more than others—either because it would have the most positive impact on your life or because it would be the easiest area to change right away to give you an experience of success? Highlight the one item that you wish to work on. For example, many people begin with something like physical health, sleep, or beginning a stress reduction program rather than choosing an item that involves another person, since that adds another element you may not be in control of. This does not mean that making more time to spend with friends and family is not a great goal; just make it open enough so that you are not stuck if one person cannot make the commitments you want to make.

Now ask yourself the most important question of this exercise:

On a scale of 1–10, with 10 being "I'm willing to move mountains to make a change in this area" and 1 being "I wouldn't be willing to lift a finger," where are you today, with this particular item? Ask yourself the question again in terms of this whole project, your own compassion fatigue, and improved self-care.

## Getting the Wake-Up Call

What would it take for you to make serious changes to your schedule and self-care routine? A health scare? The illness or death of a close family member? Going on stress leave?

When my children were very young, I remember speaking to a colleague who was in her late 50s, and she said to me: "Ah, your children are 2 and 5? I bitterly regret missing those years … you never get them back, you know. If I could do it all over again, I would not have worked full-time during those years, no matter what financial sacrifices I had to make." This comment rattled me and made me reflect on my own work/life balance. I was working 4 days a week as a crisis counselor in a very busy university counseling service and starting a private practice on the other day of the week. It was hectic in our house, and any unplanned event was overwhelming: a sick child, a visit from the electrician, anything. At the end of that academic year, I made the decision to leave my crisis counseling position and focus on my private practice with a schedule that has allowed me to exercise daily, volunteer at the children's school, make healthy meals for them, and simply have a chance to enjoy the short years of their childhood. I have never regretted this decision.

---

### *MAKING IT PERSONAL* HOMEWORK

Go back through the chapter and make sure you have completed all the activities.

In *Transforming the Pain*, Saakvitne and Pearlman propose the following reflection on your support system:

*At work:* Do you have access to a supportive group of peers? How often you do meet? If you don't currently have a peer support group, can you think of two people you could contact who would be willing to connect with you, whether in person or virtually, on a regular basis? What would you want to do with them: talk about work, go for a run, or share jokes?

*At home:* If you are in a relationship, consider having a conversation with your partner about the impact your work has on the way you behave at home. Let them know what you need when you are feeling depleted.

**RECOMMENDED READING**

Richardson, C. (1999). *Take time for your life*. New York: Broadway Books.
Posen, D. (2004). *The little book of stress relief*. Buffalo: Firefly Books.
For more books on self-care and simplifying, review the recommended readings in
Appendix C.

## Endnotes

1. Richardson, C. (1999). *Take time for your life*. New York: Broadway Books.
2. Thank you to Robin Cameron for this activity.

# Chapter 12

# Step Two, Part One: Work/Life Balance

As a work-centered culture, we've lost touch with ourselves. We skip lunch or eat on the run. Conduct business while driving our cars. Rush to pick up the kids at the end of a long day.

**—Cheryl Richardson**
*Take Time for Your Life*, p. 20

According to a U.S. study conducted by MetLife, more than half of today's employees rate work/life balance as a key job selection criterion. This is particularly true of workers between the ages of 21 and 30, who rank work/life balance ahead of financial growth and advancement.

**—Canadian Mental Health Association (CMHA)**
*"The Business Case for Work/Life Balance"*[1]

In this chapter you are invited to:

- Reflect on work/life balance
- Read Cheryl Richardson's book *Take Time for Your Life*
- Learn about Linda Duxbury's findings on work/life balance

## Work/Life Balance

A few days ago, I was running a mindfulness meditation exercise during a workshop. We were experiencing strong windstorms that day, and the whole building was howling and shaking with the wind. At some point during the meditation, we heard the siren of an emergency vehicle far off in the distance. My first thought was, "Oh, a fire truck. I guess that with all that wind, there will be fallen trees and power

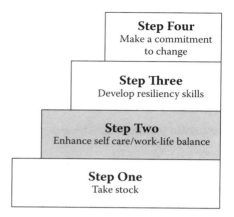

**Figure 12.1**

outages," and I then refocused on my breath and continued the meditation. When we debriefed the activity, one workshop participant, a caregiver of a person with Alzheimer's, said that her immediate thought upon hearing the siren was, "Oh no, I have to stop meditating; someone out there needs me!" Like this caregiver, most helpers are notoriously poor at self-care—maybe the worst. This is partly due to the fact that many of us were socialized to be caregivers in our families of origins and find it difficult to say no, to put ourselves first, and to make self-care a priority. I believe that the foundation of good self-care starts with good work/life balance.

Everywhere I go, I hear people complain that their lives are out of balance, and data confirm this: in North America, we spend 12 minutes per day, on average, speaking to our spouse, and 40 minutes per week playing with our children.[2]

Work/life balance is often an elusive concept, particularly for helping professionals: many helpers have very hectic shifts with few or no breaks and lead harried personal lives with numerous family commitments, errands, and chores and little time for rest and leisure activities. Helpers tend to be "on" from dawn to dusk—many of us volunteer on boards or committees during our off hours. Some of us end up married to the job with no personal lives, taking on extra work shifts and collapsing for hours in front of the television when we get home.

Granted, the concept of achieving actual "balance" may feel rather unrealistic for many of you, depending on what else is going on in your life at the moment. As a mother of a teen and a preteen who take part in competitive sports, play musical instruments, and like to be on the go, I don't claim to be the poster child for balance; but I have made some significant changes in my daily schedule, which have brought more harmony to our days and which allow for some restorative time for me. This refueling time is crucial, given the type of work I do.

## Dealing With the *Work* Part of Work/Life Balance

As a trauma counselor, one of the most effective work-related strategies that helped reduce my compassion fatigue and vicarious trauma was getting control over my schedule. Like most helpers, I am not afraid of a hard day's work, but controlling *how* that day is mapped out makes all the difference. Being in charge of my schedule meant that I no longer saw four of my most traumatized clients all in a row on a Friday afternoon (as it often seemed to happen previously). This gave me time and space to do my paperwork, attend a meeting, and process the trauma exposure from the clients I *had* seen. At the end of the week, I had seen the same number of clients as my colleagues, but I was in a much better head space, I suspect. Flexibility was the key to my well-being.

This is apparently true for many of us: in 2001, Linda Duxbury carried out a large-scale study on work/life balance in Canada. She and her staff interviewed more than 20,000 workers on ways in which they managed the competing demands from work and home. Based on this study and subsequent analyses, Duxbury concluded that one key change employers could make that would have a significant positive impact on employees' lives was flexibility of hours: "Is it easy to vary stop and end times: can you interrupt your workday and come back? Could you work at home a day a week?"[3] Being able to take a loved one to a medical appointment and then return to work ranked very high on the list.

## What If You Do Not Have Control?

I do realize that many of you who work as first responders may not have the luxury of controlling your schedule in the same way, but you can still advocate for some flexibility in your shifts (there is no harm in trying). There are some great resources available to help you make your case.

In 2009, while studying role overload among health care workers, Duxbury made the startling discovery that what dissatisfied hospital workers wanted was *not* more pay but "greater control over work hours and more respect."[4] As mentioned in an earlier chapter, she also found that one in four hospital workers was actively looking for other work. It seems to me that implementing flexible hours would cost a hospital far less than continuously replacing staff or paying for their sick leave. In their 2008 document "The Business Case for Work/Life Balance," the CMHA supports this argument: "Increasingly, managers and employers understand the importance of supporting good work/life balance among their staff. The evidence about the benefits for business is mounting and employers are increasingly implementing practices that help staff maintain a healthy balance between their work and the rest of their lives. And for good

**MORE RESOURCES**

The CMHA has produced a series of documents specifically intended for employers and managers. You can find these by going to their Web site: http://www.cmha.ca/bins/content_page.asp?cid=2-1841-1893-1898&lang=1

**RESOURCES FOR MANAGERS**

The Headington Institute is an organization that offers Web-based and in-person training and support to humanitarian relief workers across the world. Laurie Anne Pearlman is a major contributor to the institute. It provides excellent free resources for all helping professionals, regardless of whether you are an aid worker or not. I highly recommend you visit their site: www. headington-institute.com.

As part of an online course on VT, Laurie Anne Pearlman and Lisa McKay recently produced a document entitled, "Vicarious Trauma: What Can Organizations and Managers Do?"[6] It offers key recommendations to help agencies and organizations "structure work roles and develop organizational cultures that help lessen vicarious trauma in their staff." The Headington Institute very generously agreed to grant me permission to reprint this document. You can find it in Appendix A.

reason—one estimate places the cost of a lack of work/life balance at $12 billion each year."[5]

The CMHA makes key recommendations for employers in improving staff wellness and work/life balance. They are: "flexible hours, work from home where possible and appropriate, permit those returning from a leave to gradually build up to a full-time schedule, train managers on how to support work/life balance, encourage staff to stay home with sick children or elderly relatives when needed, eliminate unnecessary meetings, communicate expectations clearly to staff, and allow staff to control their own priorities as much as possible."[7]

## Dealing With the *Life* Part of Work/Life Balance

Cheryl Richardson is a life coach (and a rather famous one at that—she was the first president of the International Coaching Federation and was the team leader for the "Lifestyle Makeover Series" on the *Oprah Winfrey Show*. She also accompanied Ms. Winfrey on the "Live Your Best Life" nationwide tour). Richardson has written several excellent works on finding balance, assertiveness, and self-care. I was introduced to her book on work/life balance, *Take Time for Your Life*, by a friend about 10 years ago. This friend had been running on empty for some time. She was a clinical psychologist who had all the hallmarks of someone headed for trouble: she was carrying 90 extra pounds, was working more than 60 hours a week at her busy clinical practice, had a mortgage she could barely manage, and was feeling stressed and overwhelmed pretty much the whole time. She realized she had lost touch with herself—the successful high school athlete she used to be, the person who loved to knit and sew and do crafts and who enjoyed doing other things besides working and doing dishes and driving children to basketball practice. One element in her journey to wellness was reading *Take Time for Your Life*. My friend set realistic goals for herself (and the operative word here is *realistic*, which in turn make them achievable). Being really out of shape, she decided to start walking around the block after dinner each night. I will never forget what that was like for her: "I remember walking out 15 minutes, and turning around to hobble home in a variety of gaits to vary the pain. It took much courage and faith to keep on walking, and eventually walk-jogging in an unwieldy body, more than running for hours does now." Gradually, my friend made some big changes to her life: she downsized her home, changed her work schedule, and eventually even ran a marathon. But these changes did not happen overnight—they started with a process of taking stock of where she was, and gaining an understanding of the unhealthy patterns in her life.

Cheryl Richardson's career as a life coach emerged from her work as a tax consultant: Over time, Cheryl realized that she was helping her clients with far more than their annual returns—she was coaching them to a better life. "The time spent with clients was often very personal, requiring an intimate look into their lives. Typically, we'd talk not only about their finances (income, spending habits, and debt) but also about their medical history, family goals, and career plans. The questions they asked often concerned decisions that needed to be made about relocation, relationship conflicts, business dilemmas, or the challenge of balancing work and family."[8]

Over the years, I have spoken to many clients who realized they were being drained by massive consumer debt, a stagnant relationship, or overwhelming clutter in their homes. These were all major obstacles to "getting the life they wanted," as Cheryl puts it. As a therapist, I help clients explore the underlying reasons for these roadblocks. As a life coach, Cheryl not only challenges us to understand why we are clinging to these drains on our energy, but provides a road map to making concrete changes.

In *Take Time for Your Life*, Cheryl Richardson guides the reader through an in-depth assessment of each realm of our lives: relationships, environment, body, mind and spirit, work, and money. She urges us to assess whether we are fueling ourselves with optimal fuel or whether we are constantly running on adrenaline. She gets the reader to identify "what is draining you" and emphasizes the importance of creating a supportive community around us. For me, one of the most useful strategies in *Take Time for Your Life* was the concept of the ideal schedule.

## The Ideal Schedule

Richardson introduces the idea of creating an "ideal schedule" to help us achieve better balance. She suggests that you clear half a day per week in your schedule for time to yourself (and by the way, running errands is not considered self-care!). She acknowledges that it can be very difficult at first, and that during the first few weeks you may feel restless, guilty, or at a loss as to what to do with your self-care time. Richardson encourages readers to stick with their commitment to this self-care time even if they experience some boredom; the challenge is to see if you can learn to resist the temptation to fill up all of your free time with chores and work.

Here is my weekly ideal schedule ritual: Every Sunday morning, I sit down with my day planner and a delicious hot drink and take a look at the upcoming week. My first question is: where can I fit in *physical exercise*? I then take my planner and block off exercise time everywhere that I possibly can (the goal is to get out for a run or attend a fitness class at least three times during the workweek).

The second thing I do is look at scheduling *a fun and restorative activity*— something to look forward to. This can be a small as "rent such-and-such movie on Thursday night" or "plan dinner party"; for others it could be going to a book club, scrapbooking, or curling. It has to be something restorative that you self-define as fun. For some of us, working as helpers mean that we need to be "off" duty to unwind and the most appealing activity will be to watch a *Seinfeld* rerun in our pj's with the phone off the hook. That's okay too.

Then I look at the coming few weeks or even the next couple of months and *book some down time*. I plan ahead: If I'm going to be traveling or presenting a workshop on a Thursday, I need to have blocked off the Wednesday to prepare the workshop, get photocopies made, review my material, precook a few meals for the kids, and so forth. This may seem totally obvious to some of you, but I know some people who are continually surprised and overwhelmed by the weeks they face. I have a friend who often ends up swamped—she explained recently: "I have a week-to-week planner, so I often say yes to something without looking at the *following* week; and then when I do peek at the coming week, I realize I've booked myself to go out of town three times in 7 days and then I feel unbelievably stressed and overwhelmed." Try to look at a month at a time and then fine-tune the week ahead.

Choose someone in your life who seems to have figured out a way to fit an activity into their schedule that you wish you could do. Get the nitty-gritty details of how they made it possible.

### RECOMMENDED READING

*Take Time for Your Life* by Cheryl Richardson (1999), New York: Broadway Books.

Cheryl Richardson's book is a *must read* for any helping professional. Given that it was published in 1999, it is easiest to obtain by purchasing it online. It might be hard to find in Main Street bookstores, but you can also ask your local bookseller to order it for you.

For an excellent work/life balance inventory, complete the "What's Draining You?" inventory in Richardson's book.

***MAKING IT PERSONAL* HOMEWORK: CHERYL RICHARDSON'S IDEAL SCHEDULE**

1. Sit down with your day planner and *block off some self-care time* for the coming month (1 hour, 2 hours, half a day a week, whatever is possible for you). Write down some details about what you will do during this time.

2. *Block off some exercise time* (this can simply be a walk around the block) each week.

3. *Collect ideas from others:* A friend recently e-mailed me to say that she had finally figured out how to fit in a run in her schedule every other day. My immediate reply back to her was, "Good for you! How did you manage to fit that in? What strategy did you use to make that happen?"

# Endnotes

1. Canadian Mental Health Association (CMHA). (2008). The business case for work/life balance. Available on their Web site: http://www.cmha.ca/bins/content_page.asp?cid=2-1841-1893-1898&lang=1

2. Richardson, C. (1999). *Take time for your life*. New York: Broadway Books.

3. Duxbury, L., & Higgins, C. (2001). Voices of Canadians: Seeking work-life balance. Available online: www.hrsdc.gc.ca.

4. Duxbury, L., Higgins, C., & Lyons, S. (2009).

5. CMHA. (2008).

6. This document is part of an online course called *Understanding and Addressing Vicarious Trauma* by L.A. Pearlman & L. McKay (2008) through the Headington Institute.

7. CMHA. (2008).

8. Richardson, C. (1999). p. 3.

# Chapter 13

## Step Two, Part Two: Self-Care

In this chapter you are invited to:

- Assess your self-care
- Learn about the top 10 healthy eating resources
- Explore your compassionate voice

### Self-Care: What Works?[1]

When it comes to self-care for helping professionals, what works is deceptively simple. Have a look at the list below from Saakvitne and Pearlman's book *Transforming the Pain*:

The basics of self-care: Sleep, rest, proper diet, exercise, vacations
Renewal: Activities that replenish you
Working part-time
Nourishing activities *every day*
Access to a regular debriefing process

Now look at it again, and ask yourself the following question: How high would you currently score in each category? Do you get enough sleep on a regular basis or do you keep yourself going with caffeine? Do you eat healthily most of the time? Do you exercise for 30 minutes at least three times a week? Do you take regular vacations? Do you have access to debriefing whenever you need it? In this chapter, we will take a more detailed look at each of these and other strategies related to self-care.

## Beware of the 'Must Be Nice' Phenomenon

A co-worker announces that he is going to start swimming every day at lunch; your sister declares that she no longer has to cook suppers because her husband has decided to take care of meals now that he works part-time.

If your immediate reaction is, "Huh, *must be nice* to have that kind of time," or, "Must be nice to have that kind of help," what do you think your reaction is really about?

Have you ever been to a self-care workshop where the trim and taut presenter emphasizes the importance of eating freshly squeezed kiwi juice every morning following a 40-minute meditation practice in a private yoga studio, and you think to yourself, "Yeah, right, like that's even realistic in *my* life," and then you switch off and don't take anything in? *Must be nice* also happens a lot in the workplace, where we are so overloaded that we find it difficult to feel generous toward our co-workers' attempts at self-care.

I try to go for a run a minimum of three times a week. I find that running keeps my moods on an even keel and is a wonderful form of stress release—both emotionally and physically. I am not a particularly skilled or fast runner, but I have been running regularly for more than a decade now. However, there are times when I do not get to run for several days in a row—if I am traveling, for example. And every time I get off kilter, I know it because I start having evil thoughts about runners I see out and about. I'll see a runner and sniff, "Pfft, what a *silly* running outfit," or, "What a *ridiculous* time of the day to run." As soon as I start feeling the *must be nice* phenomenon, I know that I am actually feeling longing and envy. It's a good wake-up call that reminds me that I need to step up my self-care.

As you read through this chapter on self-care, pay attention to your inner voice. What is it telling you?

---

### GETTING ENOUGH SLEEP? TAKE THE SLEEP DEBT TEST

Try this at home—in the middle of the afternoon, go to a quiet, darkened room and lie down on the floor or couch for 10–15 minutes. If you fall asleep during this time, you have a sleep debt. (If you are a shift worker or parent of a newborn, you know this will be tough.) But many helpers who work straight days are also chronically sleep deprived. We go to bed too late (often while watching television or on the Internet), sleep poorly worrying about work and other life matters, and keep ourselves going by drinking coffee throughout the day.

Some researchers are also suggesting that the newer backlit laptops and iPads may be contributing to insomnia for those using it close to bedtime. The bright lights may interfere with the body's production of melatonin, which helps us fall asleep.[2]

**REST**

What is a restful activity for you? Is it napping, reading a novel, or watching an hour of television?

How good are you at "uni-tasking" (the opposite of multitasking)? Have you ever made a salad from start to finish without stopping midflow and doing something else (like cleaning out the crisper, checking your e-mail, or wiping the bottom of the fridge)?

I invite you to make a list of activities that are restful for you:

Now write down how often you currently do these activities in a typical week:

Now write down how often you wish you did these activities in a week.

**VACATIONS**

Recent surveys in both Canada and the United States found that many of us do not take our full vacation leave.

The sixth annual Vacation Deprivation survey, conducted by Ipsos-Reid for Expedia.ca, found 29 percent of Canadians aren't using up their allotted vacation days, giving back on average 2.43 days of unused time to their employers.

**—Reported on City News, Toronto, May 14, 2008**

A recent study in the U.S. by Orbitz, the online travel company, found a drop in the number of people taking three-week or two-week vacations and an increase in those taking a week or less. One-third of respondents said they took five or fewer days of vacation in the past year.

**—Yahoo.com, July 12, 2007**

Many respondents said that they don't have time to take time off—that the work accumulates while they are away and causes more stress when they return. Others indicated that they felt compelled to keep up with their e-mails during their holidays and were therefore rarely completely switched off from the responsibilities and concerns of work.

For a great read on this phenomenon of being chained to our desks, I recommend reading *The 4-Hour Workweek* by Tim Ferriss. Tim proposes a whole new way of looking at our workday.

## *Exercise*

Regular physical exercise is one of the best ways to manage compassion fatigue and work-related stress. In my community, one of the psychiatrists on the military base prescribes regular hot yoga classes to all of her military patients with posttraumatic stress disorder (PTSD) along with mindfulness meditation. But, although we tell our clients and patients how important physical exercise is, very few of us do it on a regular basis—it is often the first thing to go when we are overloaded.

To combat this, one busy counseling service hired a yoga instructor to come once a week to their office and everyone chipped in $10 and did yoga together at lunch. Another agency created a walking club, and that group of helpers walks outside for 30 minutes three times a week. The key to increasing physical exercise is to be realistic in the goals we set out for ourselves.

Can you think of three small ways to increase your physical activity? Take the stairs instead of the elevator, walk to the corner store when you run out of milk, go for a short walk during your lunch break. Try to make sure you exercise hard enough to sweat (the ideal would be four times a week), and do whatever activity works for you. Taking a brisk walk in your neighborhood is just fine. Whatever you do, make sure you're slightly out of breath—if you're not sweating,

---

### TESTIMONIAL: "THE LONGER I RUN, THE SMALLER MY PROBLEMS BECOME!"

*I have a high-stress job and I discovered that I needed to find a way to burn off the toxic emotional energy that permeates my days working with traumatized children and women. I understand the psychobiology of stress on the body: The fight or flight reaction sending stress hormones of cortisol and adrenaline raging throughout our system takes its toll on body and health after only a few years of repeated exposure to trauma and suffering. Scientifically the best (if not the only) way to flush out this stress reaction is to pump up the heart and activate the "feel good" hormones of dopamine and get the endorphin rush. Running has given me that ability to "burn it off!" When I run, for even 20 minutes, I begin to feel energized and I can actually feel the stress drain from my body and the weight lifting off my shoulders. It has become my passion and my salvation. Whether I run with a group of friends training for our next race, or on my own with nature and music on my iPod, I could not continue in the work that I do if I didn't have this "tool" in my box to pull out whenever I need it. I run five times per week to stay active, healthy, and, above all, resilient to continue in this very challenging and demanding, yet deeply satisfying, work. Running is my therapy!*

### —Rebecca Brown, social worker in child protection

your heart is likely not pumping very hard. Be realistic—if you don't exercise at all, aiming to walk around the block twice a week is a reasonable goal; running a 10K race in a month is not.

## Find Time for Yourself Every Day—Rebalance Your Workload

Do you work straight through lunch? Do you spend weekends running errands and catching up on your week without ever having 20 minutes to sit on the couch and do nothing? Can you think of simple ways to take minibreaks during a workday? This could simply be that you bring your favorite coffee cup to work and have a ritual at lunch where you close your door (if you have a door), sip coffee, and listen to 10 minutes of your favorite music. A friend of mine has a nap on her yoga mat at work during her lunch break. What would work for you?

Not everyone has control over their caseload, but many of us do, provided we see all the clients that need to be seen. As discussed in the previous chapter, would there be a way for you to rejig your workload so that you don't see the most challenging clients all in a row?

Make sure you do at least *one* nourishing activity each day. This could be having a 30-minute bath with no one bothering you, going out to a movie, or simply taking 15 minutes during a quiet time to sit and relax. Don't wait until all the dishes are done and the counter is clean to take time off. Take it when you can, and make the most of it. Even small changes can make a difference in a busy helper's life.

### DELEGATE: LEARN TO ASK FOR HELP AT HOME AND AT WORK

Have you ever taught a 4-year-old how to make a sandwich? How long would it take you to make the same sandwich? Yes, you would likely make it in far less time and cause far less mess in the kitchen, but at the end of the day, that 4-year-old will grow into a helpful 10-year-old, and one day, you won't have to supervise the sandwich making anymore. Are there things that you are willing to let go of and let others do their own way?

Don't expect others to read your mind: consider holding a regular family meeting to review the workload and discuss new options. Think of this: If you became ill and were in hospital for the next 2 weeks, who would look after things on the home front?

In *Take Time for Your Life*, Cheryl Richardson suggests looking to see whether there is anything you could delegate or trade your time for: organize carpooling; offer to babysit your neighbor's children in exchange for them mowing your lawn; organize a lunch-sharing program at work where you bring three people's worth of food on Monday, and then they bring you lunch for the next 2 days, and so forth.

### *Learn to Say No (or Yes) More Often*

Helpers are often attracted to the field because they are naturally giving to others; they may also have been raised in a family where they were expected to be the strong, supportive one—the caregiver. Even after we've grown up, it can be hard to stop overfunctioning for everyone.

Are you the person who ends up on all the committees at work? Are you on work-related boards? Do you volunteer in the helping field as well as work in it? Are you the crisis/support line to your friends and family? It can be draining to be the source of all help for all people. As helpers, we know that learning to say no is fraught with self-esteem and other personal issues and triggers. Do you think you are good at setting limits? If not, this is something that needs exploring, perhaps with a counselor. Can you think of one thing you could do to say no a bit more often?

Conversely, maybe you have stopped saying yes to all requests because you are feeling so depleted and burned out, resentful, and taken for granted. Have you stopped saying yes to friends, to new opportunities?

Take a moment to reflect on this question and see where you fit best: Do you need to learn to say no or yes more often?

## Healthy Eating: Top 10 Healthy Eating Resources[3]

I grew up in a home where healthy eating was important—it was the 1970s, so we had the yogurt maker, the sprouting trays, and Frances More Lappé's *Diet for a Small Planet* on the kitchen counter. But my mom was no zealot, and we still ate hot dogs and chips once in a while. There were no forbidden foods, just a focus on eating healthily most of the time. I have been primarily vegetarian since the age of 12 and have found that what I eat has a tremendous impact on my mood and overall well-being. But, during my 20s and 30s, I never really thought about the connection between healthy eating and illness. I just knew that eating pesticide-free, unprocessed foods was probably better for the planet and for me than a box of macaroni and cheese. Then, someone in my family got a scary health diagnosis and was told to clean up his act or risk having a stroke, and another relative developed type 2 diabetes. So I got to work, trying to learn more

---

**CONSIDER JOINING A SUPERVISION OR PEER SUPPORT GROUP**

Not all places of work offer the opportunity for peer support. You can organize such a group on your own (whether it be face-to-face meetings or via e-mail or phone). This can be as small as a group of three colleagues who meet once a month or once a week to debrief and offer support to one another.

about the impact of what we eat on our health. I started researching the connection between lifestyle and cancer, heart disease, and diabetes.

I know that talking about food is a touchy subject for many people. It is intrinsically connected to comfort, and for some of us, to family traditions. It is sometimes connected to shame (secret eating, struggles with our weight, disordered eating, compulsive overeating). I know, for example, that becoming vegetarian elicited very strong responses from some people in my family, who felt that by choosing this I was blaming or judging them. It can be a loaded topic.

Acknowledging that this is tricky territory, I offer you my best top 10 healthy eating resources. If this is a new area of exploration for you, I invite you to try out one or two of these. Here are a few ways to make healthy eating fun and integrate it in your daily life:

1. **Try the 5/30 challenge:** This wellness challenge is an initiative of the Heart Institute of Montreal. For the next 6 weeks, you are invited to commit to eating at least five portions of fruit and vegetable per day and exercise for at least 30 minutes daily (these can be three separate 10-minute activities such as climbing the stairs, walking to the grocery store, and going for a walk at lunch; or one 30-minute exercise session). You can make this commitment on your own or with your colleagues at work.

2. **Get a juicer:** Granted, juicers are big-ticket items (they can cost between $150 and $500), but if you add up all your fancy coffee runs, I suspect you might find that you can save up enough to buy a juicer in barely a few months. I bought myself an Omega fruit and vegetable juicer for my 40th birthday (yes, I'm a nerd) and we use it all the time. The best part has been that my children (who always resist eating enough fruit and vegetables) love making juice (and drinking it). I just make sure we have enough carrots and apples around the house all the time, and they cheerfully experiment with sticking things in the juicer. Recently we did spinach, pineapple, carrot, apple, and orange. No one liked beet juice except me, but hey, it's worth a try. My son has about 1.5 cups of fresh carrot-apple juice every morning. A juicer makes a mother happy.

3. **Try drinking green tea every day** (decaf is also fine): Green tea has been found to have powerful anticancer properties.

4. **Try a new cookbook:** I own more cookbooks than I care to admit, and the funny thing is, I use only a few of them on a regular basis (I tend to use the Internet for recipes more and more now). Of all the cookbooks I own, Bonnie Stern's *Heart Smart*[4] wins hands-down as the best "go to" cookbook for everyday healthy cooking. Every single recipe in Stern's cookbook is delicious, and you would never know that they are "healthy eating/heart smart" recipes. They are simply full of flavor and fantastic.

5. **Explore clean eating:** Clean eating is a relatively new term that refers to focusing on low salt, lean protein, complex carbohydrates, and unprocessed foods. It's not a "diet" in the sense of a weight-loss program, but

rather a way of life. I have been very impressed by the quality of the recipes in the magazine *Clean Eating*, although it has a strong emphasis on weight loss, which I do not like as much, so buyer beware. But the recipes are delicious, and again, there is no sense of being deprived or restricting what you eat. My family has given rave reviews to all the recipes in the magazine.

6. **Try a green smoothie**: Several months ago, I came across an article on the health benefits of eating raw foods. I had heard about raw foodism in the past and was always rather skeptical about this approach to nutrition. In a nutshell, raw foodism advocates eating foods in their least processed and most natural forms. The argument is that cooking food destroys important enzymes and makes foods less nutritious and less digestible. I have no idea about the science behind this, but I do know that eating mostly plant-based foods in their least-processed forms can't be a bad thing and that most of us eat far too much salt, fat, and preservatives.

   I decided to introduce more raw foods into my diet last fall, and within 2 weeks, I noticed significant changes in my overall health. After a lifetime of low-blood-sugar crashes, for once in my life, I started feeling actually satiated between meals. I no longer got that shaky, headachy feeling if I didn't get lunch right on time. I also noticed a whole host of other improvements to my overall health and energy. Eating more raw food is not about dieting or depriving yourself. Rather, it's a way of introducing more plant-based foods in your life. If you want to know more about raw food, you can read all about it at the Web sites I mention below in Raw Food Web Sites.

7. **Start taking more vitamin D:** In their book *Eating Well, Living Well: An Everyday Guide for Optimal Health,* Richard Béliveau and Denis Gingras advocate that all of us who live in the northern hemisphere should increase our vitamin D intake:

---

### TRY A GREEN SMOOTHIE!

I don't think that many people will argue with the concept that eating more greens is good for all of us. The Web site Raw Divas recommends a painless way to do this: drink a green smoothie once a day. You need a blender for this recipe: Take two ripe or frozen bananas, a handful of spinach, a cup of water, and a few ice cubes if your bananas were not frozen. Start with a little bit of spinach and add more after you are used to the taste. Try having a green smoothie at breakfast, as a midafternoon snack, or in the evening instead of your usual cookies and milk. Tera Warner of Raw Divas also has a very tasty banana ice-cream recipe on her Web site: www.therawdivas. com.

> Vitamin D … plays an absolutely essential role in calcium absorption and bone growth, as well as maintaining overall body functions. However, unlike other vitamins obtained through food, most of the vitamin D in our body (80–95%) is produced by the sun's action on the skin. … The sun's major role in vitamin D production obviously poses a problem for populations in northern countries who have much less sun exposure in the winter. … This deficiency seems to increase the risk of certain cancers. For example, the incidence of breast cancer is generally higher in regions that are far from the equator.[5]

There is some debate about how much vitamin D you should take daily, but the Cancer Society recommends 1,000 IUs during fall and winter months if you live in North America or Europe.

8. **Read Dr. Richard Béliveau's book *Foods That Fight Cancer: Preventing Cancer Through Diet*:** Dr. Béliveau is a Montreal-based biochemist. He is one of the leading researchers in the connection between nutrition, lifestyle, and cancer, with a huge interest in prevention and public education. He is the co-author of *Foods That Fight Cancer.*[6]

Through his research, Béliveau has successfully demonstrated that 75% of all cancers are lifestyle related. The main causes are smoking, nutrition (not eating enough plant-based foods, eating too much saturated fats and cured meats), obesity, and lack of physical exercise.

Béliveau believes that with a few small changes, we could dramatically reduce cancer rates that are lifestyle related. As he says in an educational video: "We wait until we have lost our health to say I should probably take care of it." "We must question ourselves about our daily decisions. It's not the foie gras or the smoked salmon you eat once a month that's a problem;

---

## RAW FOOD WEB SITES

I have no affiliation with these raw food sites but thought I would list a few that I like to visit once in a while for inspiration:

The Raw Divas Web site mentioned above has lots of recipes if you navigate around a bit.

www.rawmazing.com—I have found the best recipes on this site.

www.kristensraw.com—This site is hardcore raw vegan but offers a lot of recipes on the blog.

www.choosingraw.com has very nice lunch ideas and other recipes worth trying as well as some of the best, most balanced nutritional advice I've come across; also, not focused on weight loss.

it's the daily choices we make, the little snacks on the side that cause a problem."[7]

The solutions? Eat more vegetable-based products (fruits, vegetables, and whole grains), eat less red meat, and drink more green tea. Avoid meats cooked on high heat and bacon/cured meats. Maintain a healthy weight: "Obese individuals are 50% more likely to develop colorectal cancer (due to increased insulin and a state of chronic inflammation)," and finally, exercise regularly. Béliveau states that "regular exercise cuts cancer risks in half as it reduces insulin and inflammation" (see Endnote 7).

9. **Plan ahead:** Many meat eaters have commented that vegetarian cooking requires a lot of preparation. It's true, to some degree, that making a vegetable stew requires a lot of chopping and cooking and stirring, but many fast healthy recipes are available out there, and using a slow-cooker is a great way to have a fast, healthy meal (check out lots of recipes at the blog "A Year of Slow Cooking," crockpot365.blogspot.com). I tend to cook two or three big meals on Sundays and then we can eat healthy leftovers during the week when things are very hectic with my children's sports schedules.

10. **Be kind to yourself:** Changing the way you eat is best done in a gradual way that respects your body, schedule, and wallet. Aim to make one change a month rather than doing anything drastic. As we know, diets don't work (in fact, they make us fat—95% of all diets fail and most people gain even more weight after falling off the wagon). Improving the way you eat is a gradual process that is best done with an open mind, the willingness to experiment, and kindness toward yourself. Your body will thank you.

## A QUIET LITTLE MINDFUL SANDWICH[8]

Good-quality food is essential to fueling your body as you work in this incredibly demanding field. I don't know about you, but if I have a very challenging morning clinic where I'm working with people who are really struggling with difficult painful stories, knowing that a delicious sandwich made with focaccia bread from our local Italian deli awaits me midway through my day makes a difference to me.

And when I sit down to eat that great sandwich I am doing several things: (1) I actually am taking lunch—how many helpers skip lunch altogether? (2) I am eating something healthy and nutritious. (3) I am mindfully eating the sandwich, taking a few minutes to put everything aside and making it a meditative, quiet little sandwich.

I think that as helpers, we need to take stock of the ways in which we fuel ourselves, and food is the first obvious area to investigate.

We are seeing soaring obesity rates in our society: It comes from eating on the run, skipping breakfast, grabbing a donut for lunch and pizza for dinner—eating without really processing that we are eating. Many helpers who attend my workshops confess that they often eat in the car, while driving, on their way from one client to another.

If you would like to make some changes but aren't sure where to start, take a look at the *Chatelaine* magazine and Canadian Living Web sites. Both have a large collection of quick and healthy online recipes that can be done in 30 minutes or less.

http://www.canadianliving.com/food/quick_and_easy/
http://www.chatelaine.com/en/article/420--meals-in-minutes

I once got an e-mail from a client of mine, a tough and crusty criminal investigator who surprised and delighted his wife by researching one magazine's "quick and easy" Web site and preparing dinner for her when she got home. He confessed that he had never been to a women's magazine Web site before, but the results (quick and healthy food and his wife's reaction) had made it a great experience. He started doing this several times a week and they lived happily ever after.

## Letting the Compassionate Voice Speak[9]

I was recently sitting on the bleachers at my son's hockey game, listening to parents around me talk about their Saturday routine:

*Woman in brown turtleneck:* "We were at the arena at 7:00 a.m. today for the middle child's game, then raced back home to pick up my older child and take her to her dance lesson, then raced back home again to drive our youngest to his basketball practice. Then two of them had birthday parties in two different parts of town, and we are going out tonight so I'm not sure when I'll have a chance to even get changed!"

*Man with crew cut replied:* "I hear you; Junior had to be at soccer at 8:00 a.m. *and* we had the builders coming to fix our driveway while my older child had to be at his hockey practice. It's crazy isn't it?"

I had two reactions to this (and I hear these stories every week as I sit on the bleachers doing my people watching). My first thought came from my Critical Voice.

*The Critical Voice said:* "Tsk, tsk. These overcommitted people who enroll their kids in more than one activity, probably feeding them junk food in the car on the way from karate to swimming lessons. When will people learn to scale down? This is insane. When do they have time for themselves? Do they even get any physical exercise or is it just always about sitting on your bacon watching your kid play sports? Do they all think their kids are going to the Olympics! Tsk, tsk …"

Then, suddenly, I was visited by a totally different voice.

*The Compassionate Voice said:* "You know, those crazy years of driving children to hockey and soccer are very brief. Maybe these parents are having a wonderful time taking a few hours out of their day to sit (perhaps mindfully) and relax and watch their kids play games and have a lovely time. Maybe these parents also are really enjoying the sense of community of meeting the same parents every week and sharing stories and common experiences. Gosh, maybe some of these parents waited years to have children and went through tons of fertility treatments and maybe even adoption for the joy of watching their kids play hockey."

*Compassionate Voice continued:* "Look around you: how many parents look harried and stressed out? (My unempirical unscientific answer would be about 25%.) And what about the rest? Well, to be honest the rest of them seem to be having fun!"

No, really, I looked around on the bleachers and I saw parents talking to one another, getting involved in the management and coaching aspects of the children's sports, taking part in the sports themselves. I also saw parents enjoying their children's youth and energy and having fun watching them play sports. The dad with the crew cut had a huge smile the whole time he was at the game, and he seemed to be having a wonderful time.

What is the take-home message here? I guess it's twofold: first, that my Critical Voice is alive and well and ready to pass judgment on how people manage their time (and pass judgment on my own actions), without taking the extra step to assess the full picture, and secondly, that sometimes, Compassionate Voice doesn't get much air time.

Do you know how your Critical Voice and your Compassionate Voice react? I know that I value Critical Voice's input and it has helped me enroll my children in one—count it, *one*—sporting activity at a time instead of three. Critical Voice is also helpful in figuring out my self-care situation. But sometimes, Compassionate Voice needs to have input as well. Do you have something going on in your life right now that needs to be filtered through your Compassionate Voice?

The concept of self-care is a funny thing, particularly for people such as us Westerners who live in such an achievement-oriented society. I don't believe that you can take a diploma in self-care, post the certificate on your wall, and voila, you're done, onward and forward.

In my opinion, we are never "done" with self-care; it's not like painting our living room or some other chore on our to-do list. In fact, I would say it's more akin to making sure you eat more vegetables every day. Gobbling down three pounds of broccoli on Monday does not mean you have met all your nutritional requirements for the month (alas).

Self-care, to my mind, is something that we continually have to check in with, have conversations with, and tweak. Hence, the lovely image I carry with me about self-care is a tiny little wrench. I tinker with self-care as lovingly as the guy who works on his 1983 Fiat Spider and who never really wants it to be fixed. In fact, that's not really his goal at all. He just loves the process.

"Dig where the ground is soft" (Chinese proverb).

When I was training in couples counseling with Dr. Les Greenberg, he always used to say, "When you are working with couples, dig where the ground is soft. Work with the client who seems most ready to change, not with the client who seems most closed and defensive." So, instead of picking your trickiest area, pick the issue that you can most easily visualize improving (e.g., making a commitment to going for a walk every lunch time vs. getting rid of my difficult supervisor).

You may not notice it right away, but making one small change to your daily routine can have tremendous results in the long term. Imagine if you started walking up two flights of stairs per day instead of using the elevator, what might happen after three months?

By looking back at the different elements that have emerged through the worksheets you have already completed, you are likely coming up with strategies already. I now invite you to take the Self-Care Inventory to start honing in on specific strategies to add to your arsenal.

## THE SELF-CARE INVENTORY

Instructions:

- ✓   Check what you already do
- ○   Circle what you wish you did more often

### SELF-CARE CHECKLIST

From *Transforming the Pain: A Workbook on Vicarious Traumatization* by Karen W. Saakvitne and Laurie Anne Pearlman. Copyright © 1996 by the Traumatic Stress Institute/Center for Adult & Adolescent Psychotherapy LLC. Used by permission of W.W. Norton & Company, Inc. This selection may not be reproduced, stored in a retrieval system, or transmitted in any form or by any means without the prior written permission of the publisher.

### Physical Self-Care

- ☐ Eat regularly (e.g., breakfast, lunch, and dinner)
- ☐ Eat healthily
- ☐ Exercise
- ☐ Get regular medical care for prevention

☐ Get medical care when needed

☐ Take time off when sick

☐ Get massages

☐ Dance, swim, walk, run, play sports, sing, or do some other physical activity that is fun

☐ Take time to be sexual—with yourself, or with a partner

☐ Get enough sleep

☐ Wear clothes you like

☐ Take vacations

☐ Take day trips or mini-vacations

☐ Make time away from telephones

☐ Other:

## Psychological Self-Care

☐ Make time for self-reflection

☐ Have your own personal psychotherapy

☐ Write in a journal

☐ Read literature that is unrelated to work

☐ Do something at which you are not expert or in charge

☐ Decrease stress in your life

☐ Notice your inner experience—listen to your thoughts, judgments, beliefs, attitudes, and feelings

☐ Let others know different aspects of you

☐ Engage your intelligence in a new area (e.g., go to an art museum, history exhibit, sports event, auction, theatre performance)

☐ Practice receiving from others

☐ Be curious

☐ Say no to extra responsibilities sometimes

☐ Other:

## Emotional Self-Care

☐ Spend time with others whose company you enjoy

☐ Stay in contact with important people in your life

☐ Give yourself affirmations, praise yourself

☐ Love yourself

☐ Reread favorite books, re-view favorite movies

☐ Identify comforting activities, objects, people, relationships, places and seek them out

☐ Allow yourself to cry

☐ Find things that make you laugh

☐ Express your outrage in social action, letters, donations, marches, protests
☐ Play with children
☐ Other:

## Spiritual Self-Care

☐ Make time for reflection
☐ Spend time with nature
☐ Find a spiritual connection or community
☐ Be open to inspiration
☐ Cherish your optimism and hope
☐ Be aware of nonmaterial aspects of life
☐ Try at times not to be in charge or the expert
☐ Be open to not knowing
☐ Identify what is meaningful to you and notice its place in your life
☐ Meditate
☐ Pray
☐ Sing
☐ Spend time with children
☐ Have experiences of awe
☐ Contribute to causes in which you believe
☐ Read inspirational literature (talks, music, etc.)
☐ Other:

## Workplace or Professional Self-Care

☐ Take a break during the workday (e.g., lunch)
☐ Take time to chat with co-workers
☐ Make quiet time to complete tasks
☐ Identify projects or tasks that are exciting and rewarding
☐ Set limits with clients and colleagues
☐ Balance your caseload so no one day or part of a day is "too much"
☐ Arrange your work space so it is comfortable and comforting
☐ Get regular supervision or consultation
☐ Negotiate for your needs (benefits, pay raise)
☐ Have a peer support group
☐ Develop a non-trauma area of professional interest
☐ Other:

## Balance

☐ Strive for balance *within* your work-life and workday
☐ Strive for balance *among* work, family, relationships, play, and rest

> ### *MAKING IT PERSONAL* HOMEWORK: START A SELF-CARE IDEA COLLECTION
>
> This can be fun and you can do it with friends or at work.
>
> *With friends:* Over a glass of wine or a cappuccino, interview three friends on their favorite self-care strategies. Start making a list of ideas even if they are not ideas that you would do or can afford at the moment. Something new might emerge that you have not yet thought of.
>
> *At work:* If you are doing this at work, you could even start a contest for the best self-care idea of the week or have a "self-care board" where people post their favorite ideas. You could have a "5 minutes of self-care" at each staff meeting, where someone is in charge of bringing a new self-care idea each week.
>
> Once you have a really nice, long list, pick three ideas that jump out at you. Make a commitment to implement these in your life within the next month. Ask a friend or colleague to commit to supporting you (and you them) in maintaining your self-care goals. This could mean that they go to the gym with you every Thursday, or that they e-mail you at lunch to remind you to get out of your office. This is a wonderful way to stay on track and to validate your own experiences by sharing them.

## Endnotes

1. Mathieu, F., (2008). Part of this chapter was adapted from an article published on my blog entitled, "Top 12 self-care tips for helpers." http://compassionfatigue.ca/category/resources/articles-to-download/
2. *MSNBC Technews report*. (2010, April 28). iPad could cause insomnia researchers say.
3. Mathieu, F. (2011). This section on healthy eating is adapted from a blog post entitled, "Top ten healthy eating resources." http://compassionfatigue.ca/top-ten-healthy-eating-resources/#more-1216
4. Bonnie Stern, (2006). *Heart Smart*, Toronto: Random House Canada.
5. Béliveau, R., & Gingras, D. (2009). *Eating well, living well: An everyday guide for optimal health*. Toronto: McLelland & Stewart, p. 167.
6. Béliveau, R., Gingras, D., & Bruneau, P. (2006). *Foods that fight cancer: Preventing cancer through diet*. Toronto: McLelland & Stewart.
7. To watch a French educational video with Dr Béliveau log on to http://www.passeportsante.net/fr/audiovideobalado/
8. Mathieu, F. (2007). Adapted from an article published on my blog entitled, "A quiet little Buddhist sandwich." http://compassionfatigue.ca/a-quiet-little-buddhist-sandwich/
9. Mathieu, F. (2007). Adapted from an article published on my blog entitled, "Soccer dads, hockey moms, basketball grannies." http://compassionfatigue.ca/soccer-dads-hockey-moms-basketball-grannies/

*Chapter 14*

# Step Three: Developing CF Resiliency Through Relaxation Training and Stress Reduction Techniques

By developing the deep sense of awareness needed to care for ourselves while caring for others and the world around us, we can greatly enhance our potential to work for change, ethically and with integrity, for generations to come.

**—Laura van Dernoot Lipsky**
*Trauma Stewardship*, pp. 11–12

In this chapter you are invited to:

- Explore ways of enhancing your compassion fatigue (CF) resiliency through body awareness and other stress reduction techniques
- Learn the four steps of compassion fatigue resiliency
- Explore ways to reduce trauma exposure in your everyday life
- Learn grounding techniques to decrease your risk of developing vicarious trauma

## Developing Resiliency to the Challenging Work We Do*

The concept of resiliency is of great interest to many specialists in the field of compassion fatigue: We want to discover what protects helpers and keeps them healthy.

---

* Thank you to Robin Cameron for her help with this section.

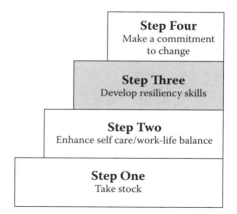

**Figure 14.1**

The solutions currently emerging from the research are simple and yet difficult to achieve: they mostly have to do with improved self-awareness and a reduction of chronic stress.

Being able to regulate your internal levels of stress can work wonders to help you cope with the stress of your highly challenging job, but how does one achieve this?

Many helpers say that they can't remember the last time they felt relaxed. Your body can only repair itself when your parasympathetic nervous system is engaged. This restorative part of the nervous system is involved in rest and digestion, and it is not properly engaged when you are worried, hurrying, fearful, angry, or anxious.

You have at your disposal the very best self-care strategy of all, and even better, you already use it thousands of times every day. Your breath is healing, restorative, and the easiest way for you to control the way that you respond to stress. Becoming more mindful of your breath and taking time out of each day to stop multitasking and just breathe gives your body and mind a much-needed chance to (literally and metaphorically) re-inspire and to vacation from chronic stress.

You can regulate your internal levels of stress through:

Developing self-awareness skills
Daily meditation, relaxation training, controlled breathing, and visualization
Trauma stewardship
Body awareness

Self-awareness is discussed in Chapter 9. Let us now take a look at three other key concepts to managing and mitigating exposure to traumatic material: mindfulness-based stress reduction (MBSR), trauma stewardship, and body awareness.

## Mindfulness-Based Stress Reduction: An Important Tool in Mitigating Compassion Fatigue in Helpers[1]

Mindfulness-based stress reduction (MBSR) is a holistic mind/body approach developed by Jon Kabat-Zinn at the University of Massachusetts Medical Center in 1979. MBSR is "based on the central concept of mindfulness, defined as being fully present to one's experience without judgment or resistance."[2] The MBSR program recommends using meditation, yoga, relaxation training, as well as strategies to incorporate these practices into everyday life.

Research on the effectiveness of MBSR is highly conclusive: more than 25 years of studies clearly demonstrate that MBSR is helpful in reducing emotional distress and managing severe physical pain. In fact, MBSR has been used successfully with patients suffering from chronic pain, depression, sleep disorders, cancer-related pain, and high blood pressure.[3] Based at Toronto's Centre for Addiction and Mental Health, Zindel Segal has developed a mindfulness-based cognitive therapy program for treating depression that has shown to be highly effective in preventing relapse.

## MBSR and Compassion Fatigue

Researchers recently turned their attention to the interaction between MBSR and compassion fatigue to see whether MBSR would help reduce CF symptoms among helpers. One study of clinical nurses found that MBSR helped to significantly reduce symptoms of CF, as well as helped the subjects be calmer and more grounded during their rounds and interactions with patients and colleagues.[4] Another study by Shapiro and colleagues investigated the effects of teaching mindfulness-based stress reduction to graduate students in counseling psychology. The study found that participants in the MBSR program "reported significant declines in stress, negative affect, rumination, state and trait anxiety, and significant increases in positive affect and self-compassion."[5]

## The Full MBSR Program

Joanne Cohen-Katz and her colleagues carried out a study of the impact of MBSR on nursing staff. This is how she describes the program: "The MBSR is taught as an 8-week program that meets approximately 2.5 hours a week and includes a 6-hour day-long retreat between the 6th and 7th weeks. Participants are asked to practice the mindfulness techniques 6 days a week as 'homework' and given audiotapes to facilitate this. Group sessions include a combination of formal didactic instruction on topics such as communication skills, stress reactivity, and self-compassion and experiential exercises to help participants integrate these concepts." Kabat-Zinn offers a detailed description of the MBSR program in his book *Full Catastrophe Living: Using the Wisdom of Your Body and Mind to Face Stress, Pain and Illness.*

As you are reading this, you may be thinking: "I don't have time to take part in a 2.5-hour, 8-week program!" Nor do you have to—let's extract the main features of MBSR and see how you might integrate them in your own life routines.

## *Incorporating MBSR Into Your Life*

The key strategies of MBSR mirror the best compassion fatigue reduction techniques described elsewhere in this workbook and how to balance the competing demands in our lives.[6]

In the Shapiro study with counseling students, five mindfulness practices were taught, adapted from Kabat-Zinn's program:[7]

1. *Sitting meditation.* This is the cornerstone of MBSR—to develop, over time, a sitting meditation that is done daily, if possible. It involves the "concentration of attention to the sensations of breathing, while remaining open to other sensory events, and to physical sensations, thoughts, and emotions."
2. *Body scan.* A very effective exercise from the field of relaxation training and stress reduction. The full version of the body scan encourages you to focus on each part of your body, one after the other, to identify where you are holding tension. This process is normally done lying down, in a quiet room. If time does not allow you to do the full scan, you can also carry out a modified version of the body scan.
3. *Hatha yoga* consists of "stretches and postures designed to enhance mindful awareness of the body and to balance and strengthen the musculoskeletal system."[8]

---

**A SHORT BODY SCAN**

Sitting in a quiet, peaceful room, close your eyes and focus on your breathing. Notice what is happening in your body: Working your way down from the top of your head, notice how your jaw, neck, and shoulders are feeling at this moment. Remember to keep breathing, and if your mind wanders, gently bring it back. If that is all the time you have, take three slow, deep breaths through your nose and gently open your eyes. If you have more time, work your way down your body, noticing how your shoulders, arms, stomach, calves, and toes feel right now.

Where to find the full body-scan exercise:

On the Web: Through Google, I was able to find several audio and scripted body scan exercises in a matter of seconds.

CD: *Creating Inner Calm* by Mark Berber (only available at Indigo/Chapters, not Amazon).

Books: *The Anxiety and Phobia Workbook,* by Edmund J. Bourne, has a body scan script as well as many other excellent resources on managing stress.

**WANT TO KNOW MORE? WHERE TO START?**

You can learn more about MBSR on your own or by taking a course or attending a workshop.

**ON YOUR OWN**

**Audio CDs**

Kabat-Zinn has produced a collection of mindfulness meditation CDs that can be purchased on his Web site and on Amazon/Indigo. Your local library may have them. Kabat-Zinn's site also has a useful FAQ that describes the different CDs and guides you on which one to buy. He has an informative blog and resources: www.mindfulnesstapes.com.

**Books**

Kabat-Zinn, J. *Full Catastrophe Living: Using the Wisdom of Your Body and Mind to Face Stress, Pain and Illness.* 1994. New York: Random House.

Kabat-Zinn, J. *Wherever You Go, There You Are: Mindfulness Meditation in Everyday Life.* 1994. New York: Hyperion.

Williams, M., Teasdale, J., Segal, Z., and Kabat-Zinn, J. 2007. *The Mindful Way Through Depression: Freeing Yourself From Chronic Unhappiness.* New York: Guilford Press.

**Video**

Kabat-Zinn offers a 1-hour stress reduction video on YouTube. Just type "stress reduction in 6 parts" in the search bar.

If you can get your hands on it, a good introduction to MBSR is offered in Bill Moyers's 1993 PBS Special "Healing and the Mind," featuring Kabat-Zinn in the Stress Reduction Clinic.

**COURSES/WORKSHOPS**

Many medium to large-sized cities offer MBSR programs several times a year. Contact your local meditation/yoga centers to see if one is being offered in your community.

4. *Guided loving-kindness meditation.* A meditation practice that focuses on developing loving acceptance toward oneself and others. You can find examples of loving-kindness meditation on the Web.

5. *Informal practices*: Exploring ways to bring mindfulness into our everyday life (while waiting in line at the grocery story, stuck in traffic, dealing with a challenging patient, etc.).

**REFLECTION**

*For me, implementing self-care strategies has been a process not an event. For the longest time, I have been interested, curious, and somehow fascinated by the practice of meditation but have always postponed my introduction to the technique. Two years ago, I attended a workshop given by a well-known practitioner in the field of self-care. In this workshop, only audio support was provided "to entertain" us for the whole day. This approach was both unique and unusual for me.*

*During the workshop, the presenter exposed the audience of 400 people to some Buddhist chants asking us to focus on our breathing and to keep our minds as open as possible. I remember how weird but audacious the exercise was and I was willing to open myself to the experience. I remember feeling this subtle wave of relaxation and warmth run thought my body. A couple of weeks later, looking to re-create this experience, I found the workshop soundtrack on YouTube. Since then, I have listened to the soundtrack regularly, mostly on workday mornings, as a little self-care ritual that supports my quest for psychological balance and inner peace as a trauma psychotherapist.*

**—Catherine Desjardins, mental health therapist**

Many wonderful resources are available to explore this concept further. I suggest that you Google the following names:

**Jon Kabat-Zinn** for more information on mindfulness meditation strategies and tapes

**Zindel Segal** to read more on the connection between mindfulness meditation and the connection to depression

**iTunes meditation** to download meditation tapes

**iTunes relaxation** to download relaxation activities of all kinds

## You Cannot Fail at MBSR

If you are new to meditation practice, the most important thing to remember is that you cannot fail at meditation. There will be times where you can meditate with ease, and other times where your mind will be racing and you will have great difficulty focusing on being mindful. You may also fall asleep. All of those are part of the process of mindfulness practice. Try not to judge your meditations. Simply try to refocus on your breath and on the meditation itself. Jon Kabat-Zinn often says, "You don't have to like it, you just have to do it." It takes time and practice but it could literally save your life.

## Trauma Stewardship: Managing Trauma Exposure

Laura van Dernoot Lipsky refers to the process of managing trauma exposure as "trauma stewardship."[9] Trauma stewardship refers to the way in which we can work with individuals in profound distress while remaining grounded in our own self-awareness: "we must respond to even the most urgent human and environmental conditions in a sustainable and intentional way."[10] This, Lipsky explains, allows us to be present for the other person's suffering without becoming overwhelmed by their pain and trauma.

To stay grounded, we need a way to process our clients' difficult experiences and make meaning of the stories we hear. We often do this by debriefing with our colleagues or close friends. However, one of the most insidious consequences of compassion fatigue is isolation from our colleagues: work overload, cynicism, and negativity in the workplace means that a lot of us have lost that crucial opportunity to debrief and support each other.

So, how to stay grounded? In her book *Help for the Helper: The Psychophysiology of Compassion Fatigue and Vicarious Trauma,* Babette Rothschild says that helpers need to find the optimal level of empathic engagement, where we are still connected with the client but where we are also not losing touch with our own body. She calls this process "body awareness." The

---

**WHAT IS THE ANS?**

The autonomic nervous system (ANS or visceral nervous system) is the part of the peripheral nervous system that acts as a control system functioning largely below the level of consciousness, and controls visceral functions. The ANS affects heart rate, digestion, respiration rate, salivation, perspiration, diameter of the pupils, micturition (urination), and sexual arousal. Whereas most of its actions are involuntary, some, such as breathing, work in tandem with the conscious mind.

**—Dorland's Medical Dictionary**
*(www.dorlands.com)*

The ANS has two branches: The sympathetic branch and the parasympathetic branch. The sympathetic branch deals with some kind of emergency or stress by controlling bodily changes that put us in a better position to fight, flee, freeze, or simply to feel frightened. For example, during sympathetic activation, our hearts beat faster, our blood pressure increases, and blood and oxygen flow to big muscles groups such as our quadriceps (and fists). After the emergency or stress situation has passed, the parasympathetic branch counters the sympathetic activation by controlling the bodily changes that lead to restoration, rest, and internal maintenance.[11]

---

concept of body awareness is particularly useful to trauma workers and helpers who are exposed to a significant amount of trauma content in the course of their work. Rothschild's work offers concrete ways of managing trauma exposure, which we will now explore.

## Understanding the Neurophysiology of Trauma Work

In *Help for the Helper*, Rothschild describes how our body and brain are deeply transformed by trauma exposure. She uses the terms "somatic empathy" and "hyperarousal" to describe how our ANS (autonomic nervous system) engages in stressful situations and in sessions where a client is recounting a traumatic event.

*Somatic empathy* means that we are empathizing with the client's story *with* our body. We may even feel physical symptoms while they are describing past trauma. An example of this is a session where a client is telling us a very graphic story of abuse and we find ourselves "in the story," our heart racing, with dry mouth and clammy hands. When that occurs, something profound also takes place in our brain, which can alter our ability to filter incoming trauma and therefore reduce our ability to protect ourselves from vicarious trauma.

We also need to pay attention to signs of *hyperarousal* in ourselves. Hyperarousal refers to a state (commonly found in individuals with post-traumatic stress disorder, or PTSD) where we are on high alert even at times when

---

### TESTIMONIAL

This story happened early in my career when I was still an MSW student. About 6 weeks into my placement at a hospital-based sexual assault treatment program, I was home alone, sleeping soundly, when I was awakened by the apartment intercom. Upon answering, a man's voice asked "Is John there?" Immediately I panicked because I was completely convinced that he had asked the question only to see if I was home alone so he could break in my door and attack me. In the midst of my panic I thought I was quite clever as I decided to stack all my canned goods in front of the door so that I could hear if he broke in. It really did not settle me because I spent a restless night having numerous nightmares. When I told my placement supervisor the next day what had happened, she stated that I needed to toughen up. The advice left me feeling minimized and to blame for what I had gone through because I had no terminology to describe or understand what I had experienced. The vicarious trauma literature did not start to surface until 5 years later. I think I survived those early years by sharing "war stories" with my peers as those were the days when we started every morning with a collegial tea.

**—Hospital social worker**

it is not necessary (that is, the sympathetic branch of the ANS isn't "switching off" as it should, even when it is no longer needed). Rothschild explains that vicarious traumatization, then, occurs when our system "goes awry" and we are unable to stop the state of persistent hyperarousal. I recall meeting a soldier with PTSD a few years ago who had recently returned from a tour of duty in Afghanistan. He spoke of the flooding of tension he would feel when stopping at red lights in our sleepy little Ontario town. When he explored this a bit more, he realized that during his tour, stopping at traffic lights or roadstops could have life-or-death consequences. His brain did not know to switch off this survival mechanism now that he was safely back home. Similarly, trauma workers who had never been in combat described having the same fears, having absorbed their clients' stories.

Rothschild argues that by increasing our self-awareness and our body awareness during sessions with clients, we can learn to reduce our vulnerability to their stories.

## How Does This Work?

Rothschild explains: "Therapist self-care requires the proper functioning of at least three neuropsychological systems: All three are necessary for the therapist to be fully in control of her own well-being even in the most distressing of situations:

1. Empathy regulation
2. ANS and arousal regulation
3. Clear thinking"

She continues: "In short, for a therapist [or, I would argue, any helping professional] to minimize risks to her emotional and physical well-being, she needs to be able to find ways to balance her empathic engagement, regulate her ANS arousal and maintain her ability to think clearly."[12]

Basically, what this means is that you need to find the optimal level of empathic engagement, where you are still connected with the client but you are also not losing touch with your own body. To learn more about this concept and strategies to mitigate the impact of trauma, I highly recommend Rothschild's book.

---

**RECOMMENDED READING**

Rothschild, B. (2006). *Help for the Helper: The Psychophysiology of Compassion Fatigue and Vicarious Trauma*. New York: W.W. Norton.
Go read, in particular, these two exercises from Rothschild's book:

Subtle moves—the handball example (pages 124–135)
Body awareness exercise (pages 107–108)

### *MAKING IT PERSONAL* HOMEWORK: DEVELOPING A DAILY PRACTICE—EVEN FOR THE BUSIEST PERSON ALIVE

Unless you have newborn triplets at home, I suspect you have a minimum of 5 minutes per day available to you for a relaxation practice. Many of us are so used to running on adrenaline (courtesy of the sympathetic branch of our ANS) that we can't relax even when we stop (if we do stop) and often give up on relaxation activities prematurely, saying they "don't work." I invite you to try this practice for one full week and then reassess its effectiveness. Choose 5–10 minutes when you are sure you will not be disturbed. This could be sitting in your car before you leave work, at home before the day begins, or at lunch hour. This breathing exercise is from a women's health Web site, but there are thousands of others available to you via the Web, iTunes, and even YouTube.

### SIMPLE DEEP BREATHING BY MARCELLE PICK, OB/GYN NP, CO-FOUNDER OF THE WOMEN TO WOMEN CLINIC IN YARMOUTH, MAINE

*The most basic thing to remember is that your breath begins with a full exhalation (I know this seems counterintuitive, but it's true). You can't inhale fully until you empty your lungs completely. It is also important to breathe in through your nose.*

*Now try this: Sit in a comfortable position with your hands on your knees. Relax your shoulders. On your next exhalation, breathe out slowly through your nose, counting to five. Tense your abdominal muscles, drawing in your diaphragm to help your lungs deflate. At the bottom of your breath, pause for two counts, then inhale slowly to the count of five. Expand your belly as you breathe in. Now close your eyes and repeat 5–10 times. Think of your diaphragm as the pump and your breath as the power.*

*If you find that your mind wanders during this exercise, don't worry. Just refocus on your counting. Some of my patients find it helpful to think of a happy color (like yellow) when they breathe in and a droopy color as they breathe out (like gray). As your awareness of your breath increases, you'll find that it becomes easier to breathe deeply without so much attention.[13]*

### PURCHASE A RELAXATION CD

Mark Berber's CD *Creating Inner Calm* breathing exercise can be purchased at Indigo stores or online.

## Making Self-Care a Priority in Our Lives

The basics of self-care are not particularly complicated. What gets in the way is the lifetime of resistance and avoidance strategies designed to keep us in denial. In addition, many of us work in very unhealthy environments that leave us depleted and overwhelmed. But in truth, once you have self-awareness, the rest is not that difficult to do. If you feel truly stuck, talking to a good therapist can be a wonderful way to start exploring this process.

## Endnotes

1.  Mathieu, F., (2009). Originally published on my blog. http://compassionfatigue.ca/category/resources/articles-to-download/
2.  Cohen-Katz, J., Wiley, S., Capuano, T., Baker, D.M., & Shapiro, S. (2005). The effects of mindfulness-based stress reduction on nurse stress and burnout, Part II: A quantitative and qualitative study. *Holistic Nursing Practice, 19*(1), 26.
3.  Cohen-Katz, J., et al. (2005).
4.  Cohen-Katz, J., et al. (2005).
5.  Shapiro, S., & Brown, K.W., & Biegel, G.M. (2007). Teaching self-care to caregivers: Effects of mindfulness-based stress reduction on the mental health of therapists in training. *Training and Education in Professional Psychology, 1*(2), 110.
6.  Shapiro, S. et al. (2007).
7.  Shapiro, S. et al. (2007).
8.  Shapiro, S. et al. (2007).
9.  van Dernoot Lipsky, L. & Burk, C. (2009). *Trauma stewardship: An everyday guide to caring for self while caring for others.* San Francisco: Berrett-Koehler.
10. van Dernoot Lipsky, L. (2009). p. 11.
11. Thank you to Dr. Susan Tasker for this.
12. Rothschild, B. (2006). *Help for the helper: The psychophysiology of compassion fatigue and vicarious trauma.* New York: W.W. Norton, p. 3.
13. Used with permission of WomentoWomen.com. © Womentowomen.com. All rights reserved.

## Chapter 15

# Step Four: Making a Commitment to Change

We cannot continue to do the work we do or to survive as a people or a society without hope. Yet, we cannot be repeatedly exposed to trauma without building up defenses against the pain and sorrow of our work. ... We cannot afford to ignore VT or to abandon hope at any level—personal, professional, or societal. Understanding VT then is essential to sustaining hope.

**—Karen Saakvitne and Laurie Anne Pearlman**
*Transforming the Pain*, p. 140

Make a formal, tangible commitment: Written, public, specific, and measurable promises of self-care.

**—Green Cross**
*"Standards of Self-Care"*

In this chapter you are invited to:

- Make a commitment to changing something concrete in your current self-care and work/life balance

Thinking about changing is easy and something most of us do dozens of times every day. We see a fit, middle-aged woman running past us and think, "I should really get in shape"; when we have a difficult day at work, we say, "Maybe I'll take that course and look for a new job"; when we have a fight with our partner, we say, "Maybe I'll call that couples counselor." So what is the difference between thinking about changing and actually making a change? Are you lazy or incompetent? Of course not; you are likely very good at coming up with ideas for others, so what's missing? What is missing is making a commitment to ourselves and planning out how it will work.

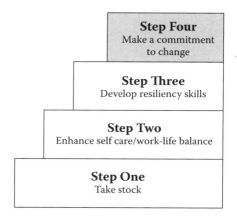

**Figure 15.1**

I now invite you to look back at the work you have done in this workbook and make a commitment to making changes in your personal and professional life that will enhance your self-care and protect you from—or mitigate your existing—compassion fatigue and vicarious trauma.

The most effective way to make lasting commitments is to share them with someone who will gently but firmly hold you accountable. Consider sharing these commitments with a friend or colleague and having a review a few months down the road.

---

### *MAKING IT PERSONAL* HOMEWORK: IDEA FACTORY

### COMMITMENT TO CHANGES I COULD MAKE IN THE NEXT ...

**Immediate plan:** Can you think of one small step you could take in the very near future to move you closer to this goal? (You could consult a friend/coach/counselor for additional ideas if you feel stuck here.)

Change I could make in the next *week*:

What do I need to get in place to make this happen?

Change I could make in the next *month*:

What do I need to get in place to make this happen?

Change I could make in the next *year*:

What do I need to get in place to make this happen?

*Chapter 16*

# Compassion Satisfaction: Reconnecting With the Rewards of the Work

> Before starting your workday, take a moment to literally stop in your tracks and ask yourself, "Why am I doing what I am doing?" After you hear your answer, remind yourself, gently, that you are making a choice to do this work. Take a deep breath; breathe in both the responsibility and the freedom in this acknowledgement.
>
> **—Laura van Dernoot Lipsky**
> *Trauma Stewardship*, p. 150

In this chapter you are invited to:

■ Reflect on the rewards of your work

In the rush of our days at the office and the many demands of our home lives, we sometimes lose touch with the reasons for which we do this work. We may no longer remember why we chose this field in the first place. In spite of its many challenges, the fact remains that working in the helping field can be a deeply rewarding experience. Many of us knew that this was what we wanted to do from an early age and cannot imagine doing any other type of work. In order to retain this love for our profession, we need to experience compassion satisfaction on a regular basis. As discussed earlier, compassion satisfaction refers to "the pleasure you derive from being able to do your work well."[1]

In *Transforming the Pain*, Saakvitne and Pearlman invite readers to explore the rewards of their work. One of the ways to do this is to reflect on what sustains us and keeps us in the field. During some of our compassion fatigue workshops, we end the day seated in a circle. Each person is asked to name one aspect of their work that they find rewarding. When people are deep in the red zone, this can be a challenging exercise and some participants will candidly say, "I'm grateful for the paycheck, for my benefits, but I can't think of anything else at the moment." Many others get a smile on their face and speak of the tremendous rewards of watching clients heal, of small victories that can have a lasting impact, of the honor they feel at being trusted with such private stories. Some helpers will mention that what is most rewarding for them is making a difference, helping others, and feeling useful. It is a deeply moving exercise that helps us reconnect with our reasons for staying in this field, after spending a day exploring its challenges.

Now it's your turn. What are the rewards of your work? What keeps you going? Please complete the following exercise.

## Reflection and Writing Exercise[2]

- What made me choose this line of work?
- What keeps me going and sustains me as a person and a professional, given the challenges of my work? (Thank you to Dr. Richard Harrison for this question.)
- What concrete strategies have made a significant difference for me and have allowed me to remain healthy and well in this career?
  - Strategies at work:
  - Strategies at home:
- If I were to do it all over again, is there anything I would do differently?
- Reflecting on successes, how have I made a difference to others?
- Can I think of a particular client whose story has profoundly touched me in a positive way? What was it about that client's story that moved me?
- Is this still the right job for me?

---

### *MAKING IT PERSONAL* HOMEWORK: INTERVIEW ON THE REWARDS OF THE WORK

Can you think of someone you know, in your field, whom you see as a particularly resilient person? Your homework is to invite this person out for coffee, or ask if you can come to their workplace, and interview them about the rewards of their work. You can use the questions above as a guide.

If you are meeting regularly with a peer support group, share your findings with your colleagues at your next meeting.

## Endnotes

1. Stamm, B.H. (Ed.). (1999). *Secondary traumatic stress: Self-care issues for clinicians, researchers, and educators* (2nd Edition). Lutherville, MD: Sidran Press, p. 12.
2. Some questions adapted from Saakvitne, K.W., Pearlman, L.A., & the staff of the Traumatic Stress Institute (1996). *Transforming the pain: A workbook on vicarious traumatization.* New York: W.W. Norton, pp. 81–85.

# Chapter 17

## Getting Help

The most insidious danger to clinicians is denial.

**—Robert Wicks**
*The Resilient Clinician*, p. 14

Over the years I have seen too many good people in the helping professions—clinicians, social workers, physicians, psychiatrists, nurses, and psychologists—go down the drain, losing careers, licenses, marriages, friends, and families because they overextended themselves and lost their way. CF, more often than not, plays a huge but unspoken role in this. I'm not trying to make excuses for unethical or unprofessional behavior, but ultimately recognizing and then rectifying all the employment/environmental factors (like the grind of constantly rotating shifts for nurses) that abet such stress in the workplace can go a long way to keep the helpers healthy for the ultimate protection of consumers and good of the general public.

**—Dr. Richard Thomas**
*Clinical psychologist*

In this chapter you are invited to:

- Review the key elements of compassion fatigue (CF) and vicarious traumatization (VT)
- Read more on compassion fatigue therapy and how it works
- Reflect on getting help when you need it

## Quick Review of the Key Elements of CF/VT

Compassion fatigue and vicarious trauma are normal occupational hazards of the work of helping others: we get CF, VT, or both because we care.

Compassion fatigue can contaminate a workplace as a whole as well as individual staff.

Your signs and symptoms *are* your warning signs and can also be the place to begin implementing strategies.

The solutions lie in reducing your isolation; taking a long, hard look at your workload; managing stressful experiences with relaxation and breathing techniques; and finally, making self-care your number one priority.

Not all workplaces were created equal. You could be experiencing job burn-out due to an unsupportive workplace in addition to the challenging work that you do with clients and patients. Put your job on probation until your organization can demonstrate that they can help protect you from the most damaging aspects of CF/VT. As Cheryl Richardson says, "We all have choices. Some of them may be very difficult … but don't confuse tough choices with no choices."[1]

## What If Those Strategies Are Not Enough?

Compassion fatigue can lead to very serious problems such as depression, anxiety, and suicidal thoughts. If this happens, talk to your physician about options such as counseling or consider contacting your EAP (employee assistance program) or a therapist in your community. When looking for a counselor, be sure to ask them if they are familiar with treating compassion fatigue.

In addition to the strategies described above, there are effective treatment modalities available to helpers with more severe compassion fatigue. Compassion fatigue counseling needs to focus on a combination of screening for and treating depression and secondary traumatic stress as well as developing an early detection system to prevent relapse. The focus is also on assessing work/life balance and developing strategies to deal with difficult caseloads and repeated exposure to traumatic material. I recommend reading Charles Figley's, Beth Stamm's, and Karen Saakvitne and Laurie Anne Pearlman's books for more information on this (a complete list of recommended reading is available in Appendix C).

## How Do You Feel About Getting Help?

A stigma still seems to surround the idea of accessing personal counseling, even among mental health professionals themselves. If you want help but are unsure where to turn, I recommend starting with word of mouth: ask a trusted colleague or friend for a recommendation. Your family physician may also have a list of practitioners in the community. Be ready to shop around—the first person you meet may not be a good fit. For some of us, it can be financially prohibitive to pay for psychotherapy. Check if your workplace has access to an EAP (employee assistance program), which usually provides short-term counseling free of charge. Ask the EAP referral office whether you are allowed to continue seeing the counselor after the sessions have expired (by paying out of your own pocket). It can be very frustrating to have found someone you trust and feel comfortable with, only to have your time run out. If you do not have EAP, check whether your community has a community mental health center that provides counseling on a sliding scale.

If you consult your family doctor, ask them whether they are familiar with compassion fatigue and burnout. They may not have heard of these terms and may diagnose you with depression and prescribe antidepressants without a thorough assessment of the factors contributing to your low mood. In some cases, being on medication may help—but if your workplace stress isn't addressed, nothing will really change and your situation may not improve.

### WHAT IS THE DIFFERENCE BETWEEN PSYCHIATRISTS, PSYCHOLOGISTS, AND PSYCHOTHERAPISTS?

*Psychiatrists* are medical doctors who have specialized training in psychiatry. They can prescribe medication and normally see patients with more severe psychiatric difficulties (posttraumatic stress disorder, bipolar disorder, schizophrenia, severe depression) as well as assess individuals with less severe problems for medication. In my experience, many psychiatrists have very heavy caseloads and do not have a great deal of time to spend with their patients. A typical follow-up appointment may be 10–15 minutes in length every 2 months to monitor your medication.[2] Some psychiatrists do offer longer sessions and talk therapy, but they are hard to find. In Canada, psychiatrists are covered by Medicare and are therefore free of charge.

*Psychologists* are professionals with a master's degree or a PhD (it depends on where you live) in psychology. There are many different kinds of psychologists but the ones who are qualified to offer counseling are clinical psychologists and have to be licensed by a regulatory body (usually a state or provincial board) to practice. Psychologists can diagnose patients and perform psychological tests (e.g., to assess someone for a learning disability, or ADHD, or following a stroke) but they cannot prescribe medication (except in certain U.S. states). Many psychologists work in private practice or for a school or hospital and offer both psychometric testing and talk therapy. They must declare areas of competency and not work outside of their scope of practice (a child psychologist cannot start seeing adults without being authorized to do so, etc.). Psychologists in private practice are not normally covered by Medicare, but many health insurance plans offer a certain amount of coverage per year for psychological services. Check with your provider for more details.

*Psychotherapist* is not a regulated term (although some provinces such as Nova Scotia and Ontario and some states are working towards regulation). In the province of Quebec, it is a restricted term, which means that you must have been approved by a certification body to call yourself a psychotherapist. In most states and provinces, it can refer to anyone who provides counseling, including psychiatrists and psychologists, social workers, and mental health counselors. But it can also be used by anyone else who wants to put on a sham—in my community, we recently had someone (who turned out to be a con artist) open an office stating that he was an "anxiety expert and former psychologist." There was little anyone could do because he did not belong to a regulatory body. This is why it is always a good idea to ask your physician or a trusted friend for a referral rather than pick someone from the Yellow Pages.

Many mental health counselors use the term psychotherapist and are also fully certified by a regulatory body. For example, in Ontario, registered social workers belong to the Ontario College of Social Work and have to adhere to a code of practice and fulfill some educational and training requirements before receiving their license. I am a Certified Mental Health Counselor with the Canadian College of Counselors and Psychotherapists and had to do the same.

Some psychotherapists are covered by supplemental health insurance, but some are not. Make sure you ask the counselor about this if you are concerned about your ability to pay.

If you are confused, you're not alone. For an excellent discussion on the difference between terms and qualifications, I recommend you visit Dr. Suzanne Lacombe's Web site, http://www.myshrink.com, and look for the articles entitled "How to Choose a Therapist" and "What Is a Psychotherapist?"

## Compassion Fatigue Therapy and How It Works

Now for the good news: Individuals with compassion fatigue normally respond very rapidly to improvements in their self-care and work/life balance. Anna Baranowsky and Eric Gentry are psychologists who developed what they call the Accelerated Recovery Program (ARP) for treating compassion fatigue in helpers. They have proposed five areas for treating CF[3]:

1. **Resiliency skills:** Rebounding from life and work difficulties and strengthening areas of our lives to cushion the fall when the going gets rough. Resiliency skills also include developing a mindfulness practice and protecting ourselves from trauma content, as discussed in earlier chapters.
2. **Skills acquisition:** What symptoms are being caused by areas of work where you do not have adequate training?

I invite you to assess where you are at in each of these five areas.

Then, pick one area that you want to focus on. I encourage you to focus on the area that seems the most *realistic* and *achievable*. Far too often, we focus on the area of our life that feels the most out of control or overwhelming. This rarely results in success because we rapidly get discouraged when the challenge seems insurmountable. If you had to clean your entire basement or the "everything" drawer in your kitchen, which one would you be more likely to successfully accomplish?

3. **Self-care:** What symptoms are caused by the professional overextending themselves in their work or personal lives? Do you have self-soothing skills, good boundaries?
4. **Internal conflicts:** Unresolved personal issues, knowing what we need to do yet being unable to do it (e.g., physical exercise, proper eating).
5. **Connection with others:** Social support both at work and at home is essential to sustaining ourselves, as we've discussed earlier.

## Conclusion

Here is an e-mail I recently received from a former emergency room nurse, who had just attended a one-day compassion fatigue workshop that I had offered in her community:

> *I wanted to extend my appreciation for the opportunity to hear you speak. I was truly captivated. I could have been the only person in the room, and you were speaking directly to me. The workshop was very reflective, and painful for me at times. I had a few tears a couple of times. I was able to realize how desperately I had struggled and how much I have healed. I do not regret my experiences. I know during those times I have brought people great comfort. I have decided to feel honored that I was chosen to cross the path of those who have suffered great loss through trauma. I am truly passionate about bringing awareness to nursing leadership so we may be able to care better for those who care for others.*

So, in closing, I will repeat the words of this dedicated nurse and say that this workbook will hopefully offer you some tools "so we may be able to care better for those who care for others." If you have any questions or comments, I invite you to get in touch with me: whp@cogeco.ca.

**—Françoise Mathieu**

***MAKING IT PERSONAL* HOMEWORK**

Have a look through the recommended readings in Appendix C and identify a few resources that may be useful to you. If you are part of a support group, you can share the books with each other to reduce costs. You can also visit your local library and see if they have them in stock. If they do not, ask them to order the books—they may agree to purchase them for their collection.

# Endnotes

1. Richardson, C. (1999). *Take time for your life*. New York: Broadway Books, p. 54.
2. For a fascinating albeit controversial read on the challenge facing psychiatrists in the era of managed care and big pharma, I recommend that you read *Unhinged* by Daniel Carlat. Carlat, Daniel. (2010). *Unhinged: The trouble with psychiatry—A doctor's revelations about a profession in crisis*. New York: Free Press.
3. Gentry, J.E., Baranowsky, A.B., & Dunning, K. (1997). *Accelerated recovery program for compassion fatigue*. Paper presented at the meeting of the International Society for Traumatic Stress Studies, Montreal, Quebec, Canada.

# Appendix A

## Vicarious Trauma: What Can Organizations and Managers Do?

Excerpted by CARE from *Understanding and Addressing Vicarious Trauma*. L.A. Pearlman and L. McKay (2008). Headington Institute, www.headington-institute.org. Reprinted with permission.

Some humanitarian workers feel that their own organization increases their vicarious trauma instead of helping reduce it! Your organization's policies and practices may be frustrating and make things feel unnecessarily complicated. But it's worth remembering that organizations and managers don't deliberately set out to make life more difficult for you and the people you are trying to help. Sometimes they don't make the best use of the limited time and resources available to them, and this impedes your ability to do your job as well as you'd like. Sometimes they are just facing many competing demands and don't have enough time or resources to do everything with the greatest care and consideration.

However, when humanitarian organizations take an active interest in staff well-being they take a big step toward addressing things that can contribute to vicarious trauma.

*Even in crisis situations there is a lot that organizations and management can do to structure work roles and develop organizational cultures that help lessen vicarious trauma in their staff.*

### Basic Considerations for Organizations

Here are some basic considerations for organizations. These can lessen the risk of vicarious trauma by helping humanitarian workers feel supported, valued, competent, and connected:

1. Adequate salary and time off (including R&R) for all staff;
2. Sufficient orientation, professional training, and management supervision for staff to feel competent and supported in their jobs;
3. Plans for staff safety (including security training and briefing on security protocols);

4. Access to medical and mental health support services including:
   - Health insurance
   - Information/training about the psychological and spiritual hazards of the work and effective self-care
   - Access to good confidential counseling support as needed; and
5. Support for families around issues such as child care, separation and relocation.

## *Organizational Culture and Work Roles*

In addition, humanitarian workers will benefit from an organizational culture and work roles that are structured in ways that help prevent vicarious trauma by:

1. Encouraging connections, morale, and relationships, perhaps through some or all of the following:
   - Working in teams
   - Providing other avenues to connect with colleagues (e.g., social activities such as having lunch or occasional outings together)
   - Developing peer support networks
2. Encouraging communication and staff contributions by:
   - Providing a voice in decision-making from and feedback to staff at all levels of the organizational hierarchy
   - Providing information to help staff understand how and why decisions about resource allocations, deadlines, policies, and assignments are made
   - Looking for ways to build diversity and job enrichment into the work
   - Allowing for and actively encouraging staff to take adequate breaks during work

---

**THINK ABOUT IT**

- What are some things your organization already does well to support its staff and help reduce the risk of vicarious trauma?
- Are there some practical things you can think of that your organization could do better to support staff and reduce the risk of vicarious trauma:
  - During recruitment?
  - During orientation?
  - During employment?
- Upon leaving the organization?

## *What Managers Can Do*

Are you a manager? Managers can take many steps to help lessen the impact of vicarious trauma on staff they are supervising. Here are some of them.

1. Understand the psychological and spiritual impact of humanitarian work:
   - Be alert to how the cumulative exposure to stressful and traumatic situations may be affecting staff.
   - Regularly check in with staff about how they're coping—do not wait for them to approach you with a problem.
   - Support staff in seeking counseling or coaching if and when needed.
2. Set a good example in the way that you care for yourself, including:
   - Work at a sustainable and reasonable pace over time, and encourage staff you supervise to do the same
   - Openly value things and people outside of work (e.g., time spent with your family)
   - Take allocated leave time
   - Acknowledge that humanitarian work can be challenging and that healthy work/life balance takes practice and intentionality.
3. Especially during times of increased pressure or crises, look for ways to help staff keep current challenges in perspective by:
   - Reminding staff of the bigger picture of the organization's mission and purpose, and how this assignment or disaster response fits into that bigger picture
   - And reminding staff of the value the organization places upon them both as people and the organization's most important resources—the staff. Encourage the staff to work in sustainable ways. If that does not appear possible in the short-term, encourage them to take extra time after the immediate impact phase is over to rest and regain equilibrium.
4. Express concern for the general well-being of your staff and not just the quality of the work they are doing.
5. Make sure that staff suggestions and feedback about their jobs and the organization are heard and valued—even if you are fairly sure they will not result in tangible change in the near future.
6. Do not say or do things that would stigmatize staff who are struggling with vicarious trauma or other stress or trauma-related issues.
7. Strive to stay positive, and to praise and acknowledge effort and results whenever possible.

*Managers can do many things to help lessen the impact of vicarious trauma on staff they are supervising, including being a good example in how they maintain and care for themselves.*

**THINK ABOUT IT**

■ If you are a manager, what are some things you do well to help lessen the impact of vicarious trauma on your staff? If you aren't a manager, what does your manager do well?

■ If you are a manager, what conversations could you have with your staff that would help them identify ways to cope with and transform vicarious trauma?

■ What are some things you as a manager (or your manager) could do better to help lessen the impact of vicarious trauma?

# Appendix B

## Standards of Self-Care Guidelines

Green Cross Academy of Traumatology

**Reprinted with permission. www.greencross.org**

### I. Purpose of the Guidelines

As with the standards of practice in any field, the practitioner is required to abide by standards of self-care. These Guidelines are utilized by all members of the Green Cross. The purpose of the Guidelines is twofold: First, do no harm to yourself in the line of duty when helping/treating others. Second, attend to your physical, social, emotional, and spiritual needs as a way of ensuring high quality services for those who look to you for support as a human being.

### II. Ethical Principles of Self-Care in Practice

These principles declare that it is unethical not to attend to your self-care as a practitioner because sufficient self-care prevents harming those we serve.

1. Respect for the dignity and worth of self: A violation lowers your integrity and trust.
2. Responsibility of self-care: Ultimately it is your responsibility to take care of yourself and no situation or person can justify neglecting it.
3. Self-care and duty to perform: There must be a recognition that the duty to perform as a helper cannot be fulfilled if there is not, at the same time, a duty to self-care.

### III. Standards of Humane Practice of Self-Care

1. Universal right to wellness: Every helper, regardless of her or his role or employer, has a right to wellness associated with self-care.
2. Physical rest and nourishment: Every helper deserves restful sleep and physical separation from work that sustains them in their work role.
3. Emotional rest and nourishment: Every helper deserves emotional and spiritual renewal both in and outside the work context.
4. Sustenance modulation: Every helper must utilize self restraint with regard to what and how much they consume (e.g., food, drink, drugs, stimulation) since it can compromise their competence as a helper.

### IV. Standards for Expecting Appreciation and Compensation

1. Seek, find, and remember appreciation from supervisors and clients: These and other activities increase worker satisfactions that sustain them emotionally and spiritually in their helping.
2. Make it known that you wish to be recognized for your service: Recognition also increases worker satisfactions that sustain them.
3. Select one or more advocates: They are colleagues who know you as a person and as a helper and are committed to monitoring your efforts at self-care.

### V. Standards for Establishing and Maintaining Wellness

#### Section A: Commitment to self-care

1. Make a formal, tangible commitment: Written, public, specific, and measurable promises of self-care.
2. Set deadlines and goals: The self-care plan should set deadlines and goals connected to specific activities of self-care.
3. Generate strategies that work and follow them: Such a plan must be attainable and followed with great commitment and monitored by advocates of your self-care.

#### Section B: Strategies for letting go of work

1. Make a formal, tangible commitment: Written, public, specific, and measurable promise of letting go of work in off hours and embracing rejuvenation activities that are fun, stimulating, inspiriting, and generate joy of life.
2. Set deadlines and goals: The letting go of work plan should set deadlines and goals connected to specific activities of self-care.

3. Generate strategies that work and follow them: Such a plan must be attainable and followed with great commitment and monitored by advocates of your self-care.

### Section C: Strategies for gaining a sense of self-care achievement

1. Strategies for acquiring adequate rest and relaxation: The strategies are tailored to your own interest and abilities which result in rest and relaxation most of the time.
2. Strategies for practicing effective daily stress reductions method(s): The strategies are tailored to your own interest and abilities in effectively managing your stress during working hours and off-hours with the recognition that they will probably be different strategies.

## VI. Inventory of Self-Care Practice—Personal

### Section A: Physical

1. Body work: Effectively monitoring all parts of your body for tension and utilizing techniques that reduce or eliminate such tensions.
2. Effective sleep induction and maintenance: An array of healthy methods that induce sleep and a return to sleep under a wide variety of circumstances including stimulation of noise, smells, and light.
3. Effective methods for assuring proper nutrition: Effectively monitoring all food and drink intake and lack of intake with the awareness of their implications for health and functioning.

### Section B: Psychological

1. Effective behaviors and practices to sustain balance between work and play
2. Effective relaxation time and methods
3. Frequent contact with nature or other calming stimuli
4. Effective methods of creative expression
5. Effective skills for ongoing self-care
   a. Assertiveness
   b. Stress reduction
   c. Interpersonal communication
   d. Cognitive restructuring
   e. Time management
6. Effective skill and competence in meditation or spiritual practice that is calming
7. Effective methods of self assessment and self-awareness

## Section C: Social/interpersonal

1. Social supports: At least five people, including at least two at work, who will be highly supportive when called upon
2. Getting help: Knowing when and how to secure help—both informal and professional—and the help will be delivered quickly and effectively
3. Social activism: Being involved in addressing or preventing social injustice that results in a better world and a sense of satisfaction for trying to make it so

## VII. Inventory of Self-Care Practice—Professional

1. Balance between work and home: Devoting sufficient time and attention to both without compromising either.
2. Boundaries/limit setting: Making a commitment and sticking to it regarding:
   a. Time boundaries/overworking
   b. Therapeutic/professional boundaries
   c. Personal boundaries
   d. Dealing with multiple roles (both social and professional)
   e. Realism in differentiating between things one can change and accepting the other
3. Getting support/help at work through
   a. Peer support
   b. Supervision/consultation/therapy
   c. Role models/mentors
4. Generating work satisfaction: By noticing and remembering the joys and achievements of the work

## VIII. Prevention Plan Development

1. Review current self-care and prevention functioning
2. Select one goal from each category
3. Analyze the resources for and resistances to achieving goal
4. Discuss goal and implementation plan with support person
5. Activate plan
6. Evaluate plan weekly, monthly, yearly with support person
7. Notice and appreciate the changes

# Appendix C

## Additional Recommended Books

### Assertiveness

Alberti, R.E. & Emmons, M.L. (2008). *Your perfect right: Assertiveness and equality in your life and relationships* (9th ed.). Atascadero, CA: Impact.

### Anxiety

Antony, M.M., & McCabe, R.E. (2004). *10 simple solutions to panic: How to overcome panic attacks, calm physical symptoms, and reclaim your life.* Oakland, CA: New Harbinger.

Antony, M.M., & Norton, P.J. (2009). *The anti-anxiety workbook: Proven strategies to overcome worry, panic, phobias, and obsessions.* New York: Guilford Press.

Antony, M.M., & Swinson, R.P. (2009). *When perfect isn't good enough: Strategies for coping with perfectionism* (2nd ed.). Oakland, CA: New Harbinger.

Greenberger, D., & Padesky, C.A. (1995). *Mind over mood: Change how you feel by changing the way you think.* New York: Doubleday.

### Compassion Fatigue/Vicarious Trauma

Figley, C.R. (Ed.). (1995). *Compassion fatigue: Coping with secondary traumatic stress disorder in those who treat the traumatized.* New York: Brunner/Mazel.

Figley, C.R. (Ed.). (2002). *Treating compassion fatigue.* New York: Brunner/Routledge.

Gentry, E. (2002). Compassion fatigue: A crucible of transformation. *Journal of Trauma Practice, 1*(3/4), 37–61.

Killian, K. (2008). Helping till it hurts? A multimethod study of compassion fatigue, burnout, and self-care in clinicians working with trauma survivors. *Traumatology, 14*(2), 32–44.

Pearlman, L.A., & Saakvitne, K.W. (1995). *Trauma and the therapist: Countertransference and vicarious traumatization in psychotherapy with incest survivors.* New York: W.W. Norton.

Saakvitne, K.W., Pearlman, L.A., & the staff of the Traumatic Stress Institute (1996). *Transforming the pain: A workbook on vicarious traumatization.* New York: W.W. Norton.

Stamm, B.H. (Ed.). (1999). *Secondary traumatic stress: Self-care issues for clinicians, researchers, and educators* (2nd Ed.). Lutherville, MD: Sidran Press.

## Creativity

Robinson, K., & Aronica, L. (2009). *The element: How finding your passion changes everything.* New York: Viking.

## Chronic Stress

Maté, G. (2003). *When the body says no: The cost of hidden stress.* Toronto: Random House.

## Couples Counseling

Gottman, J., & Silver, N. (1999). *Seven principles for making marriage work.* New York: Random House.

Weiner Davis, M. (2003). *The sex-starved marriage: A couple's guide to boosting their marriage libido.* New York: Simon & Schuster.

## Depression

Greenberger, D., & Padesky, C.A. (1995). *Mind over mood: Change how you feel by changing the way you think.* New York: Doubleday.

Williams, M.G., Teasdale, J.D., Segal, Z., & Kabat-Zinn, J. (2007). *The mindful way through depression: Freeing yourself from chronic unhappiness.* New York: Guilford Press.

## Getting Organized

Morgenstern, J. (1998). *Organizing from the inside out: The foolproof system for organizing your home, your office, and your life.* New York: Henry Holt and Co.

Morgenstern, J. (2004). *Never check e-mail in the morning and other unexpected strategies for making your work life work.* New York: Fireside.

## Mindfulness

Nhat Hanh, T. (2009). *Happiness: Essential mindfulness practices.* Berkeley, CA: Parrallax Press.

Ricard, M. (2010). *Why meditate? Working with thoughts and emotions.* New York: Hay House.

## Money/Working Part-time

Baxter, A., Self, A., Dunsworth, K., Gunn, R., & Hanna, S. (2009). *The smart cookies' guide to making more dough: How five young women got smart, formed a money club, and took control of their finances.* Toronto, Ontario, Canada: Delta.

Dominguez, J., & Robin, V. (2008). *Your money or your life: Transforming your relationship with money and achieving financial independence. Third edition revised for the 21st century.* New York: Penguin Books.

Frankel, L. (2005). *Nice girls don't get rich: 75 avoidable mistakes women make with money.* New York: Warner Books.

Vaz Oxlade, G. (2009). *Debt-free forever: Take control of your money and your life.* Toronto, Ontario, Canada: HarperCollins.

## Self-Care/Stress Reduction

Borysenko, J. (2001). *Inner peace for busy people.* Carlsbad, CA: Hay House.

Domar, A. (2000). *Self-nurture: Learning to care for yourself as effectively as you care for everyone else.* New York: Penguin Books.

O'Hanlon, B. (1999). *Do one thing different: Ten simple ways to change your life.* New York: HarperCollins.

Posen, D. (2004). *The little book of stress relief.* Buffalo, NY: Firefly Books.

Ricard, M. (2010). *Why meditate? Working with thoughts and emotions.* New York: Hay House.

Sapolsky, R.M. (2004). *Why zebras don't get ulcers* (3rd ed.). New York: Holt.

Rothschild, B. (2006). *Help for the helper: The psychophysiology of compassion fatigue and vicarious trauma.* New York: W.W. Norton.

Weiss, L. (2003). *The therapist's guide to self-care.* New York: Brunner-Routledge.

## Simplifying

Fanning, P., & Mitchener, H.G. (2001). *50 best ways to simplify your life.* Oakland, CA: New Harbinger.

Ferriss, T. (2004). *The 4-hour workweek.* New York: Random House.

St. James, E. (1994). *Simplify your life: 100 ways to slow down and enjoy the things that really matter.* New York: Hyperion.

St. James, E. (2001). *Simplify your work life: Ways to change the way you work so you have more time to live.* New York: Hyperion.

## Trauma/Addictions

Herman, J.L. (1992). *Trauma and recovery.* New York: Basic Books.

Levine, P. (1997). *Waking the tiger: Healing trauma.* Berkeley, CA: North Atlantic Books.

Maté, G. (2008). *In the realm of the hungry ghosts: Close encounters with addiction.* Toronto, Ontario, Canada: Vintage Canada.

## Work/Life Balance

Gahrmann, N. (2002). *Succeeding as a superbusy parent.* Haverford, PA: Infinity Publishing.

Martin, L. (2004). *Briefcase moms: 10 proven practices to balance working mothers' lives.* North Vancouver, British Columbia, Canada: Cornerview Press.

Richardson, C. (1999). *Take time for your life.* New York: Broadway Books.

Schwartz, T. (2010). *The way we're working isn't working.* New York: Free Press.

Sinetar, M. (1987). *Do what you love and the money will follow.* New York: Random House.

# Bibliography

Baranowsky, A. (2002). The silencing response in clinical practice: On the road to dialogue. In C.R. Figley (Ed.), *Treating compassion fatigue*. New York: Brunner/Routledge, pp. 155–170.

Courtois, C.A., & Ford, J.D. (2009). *Treating complex traumatic stress disorders*. New York: Guilford Press.

Figley, C.R. (Ed.). (1995). *Compassion fatigue: Coping with secondary traumatic stress disorder in those who treat the traumatized*. New York: Brunner/Mazel.

Figley, C.R. (Ed.). (2002). *Treating compassion fatigue*. New York: Brunner/Routledge.

Gentry, E. (2002). Compassion fatigue: A crucible of transformation. *Journal of Trauma Practice, 1*(3/4), 37–61. Note: To obtain a PDF of this article, simply Google "Gentry crucible of transformation" and download the article from his Web site: www.compassionunlimited.com. (For some reason, visiting his Web site directly does not work but using Google does.) Do not download the version from Gift From Within as it is not the complete article.

Killian, K. (2008). Helping till it hurts? A multimethod study of compassion fatigue, burnout, and self-care in clinicians working with trauma survivors. *Traumatology, 14*(2), 32–44.

McCann, I.L., & Pearlman, L.A. (1990). Vicarious traumatization: A framework for understanding the psychological effects of working with victims. *Journal of Traumatic Stress, 3*, 131–149.

Pearlman, L.A., & Saakvitne, K.W. (1995). *Trauma and the therapist: Countertransference and vicarious traumatization in psychotherapy with incest survivors*. New York: W.W. Norton.

Remen, R.N., (1996). *Kitchen table wisdom*. New York: Riverhead Books.

Richardson, J. (2001). *Guidebook on vicarious trauma: Recommended solutions for anti-violence workers*. Ottawa, Ontario, Canada: National Clearinghouse on Family Violence.

Rothschild, B. (2006). *Help for the helper: The psychophysiology of compassion fatigue and vicarious trauma*. New York: W.W. Norton.

Saakvitne, K.W., & Pearlman, L.A. (1995). Treating therapists with vicarious traumatization and secondary traumatic stress disorders. In C. Figley (Ed.), *Compassion fatigue: Coping with secondary traumatic stress disorder in those who treat the traumatized*. New York: Brunner/Mazel, pp. 150–177.

Saakvitne, K.W., Pearlman, L.A., & the staff of the Traumatic Stress Institute (1996). *Transforming the pain: A workbook on vicarious traumatization*. New York: W.W. Norton.

Stamm, B.H. (Ed.). (1999). *Secondary traumatic stress: Self-care issues for clinicians, researchers, and educators* (2nd Ed.). Lutherville, MD: Sidran Press.

van Dernoot Lipsky, L. & Burk, C. (2009). *Trauma stewardship: An everyday guide to caring for self while caring for others.* San Francisco: Berrett-Koehler.

# Index

# About the Author

**Françoise Mathieu** holds a master's degree in counseling psychology. She is a certified mental health counselor with the Canadian Counselling and Psychotherapy Association and a compassion fatigue specialist. Her experience stems from more than 15 years as a counselor, working in various community mental health environments including crisis response, a university student center, and with law enforcement staff. She has worked extensively with military personnel, offering trauma support and couples and individual counseling to soldiers and their families.

Since 2001, Françoise has given hundreds of seminars on compassion fatigue and vicarious trauma across the country to thousands of helping professionals in the fields of health care, trauma services, law enforcement, education, community health, and addictions.

She lives in Kingston, Ontario, with her partner and her two children.